GUITAR WORLD

PRESENTS

Dear

GUITAR
HERO

GUITAR WORLD
PRESENTS

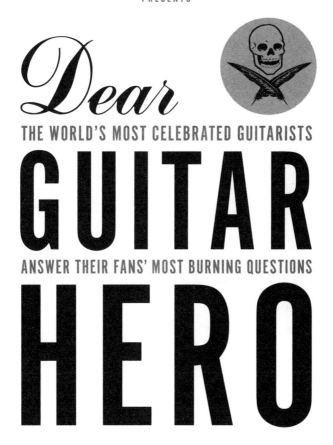

Dear

THE WORLD'S MOST CELEBRATED GUITARISTS

GUITAR

ANSWER THEIR FANS' MOST BURNING QUESTIONS

HERO

Backbeat
Books

AN IMPRINT OF HAL LEONARD CORPORATION

Published in 2012 by Backbeat Books
An Imprint of Hal Leonard Corporation
7777 West Bluemound Road
Milwaukee, WI 53213

Trade Book Division Editorial Offices
33 Plymouth St., Montclair, NJ 07042

Printed in the United States of America

Executive Producer: Brad Tolinski
Editors: Jeff Kitts, Brad Tolinski, Chris Scapelliti, Brad Angle
Art Director: Alexis Cook
Photo Editor: Jimmy Hubbard

Library of Congress Cataloging-in-Publication data is available upon request.

ISBN 978-1-61713-039-7

www.backbeatbooks.com

CONTENTS

GUITAR WORLD

PRESENTS

Dear

GUITAR
HERO

DEAR GUITAR HERO

ACE
FREHLEY

Q: **Where did you get the idea for the smoking guitar? How did you make it work? And did it ever get out of hand and cause serious damage?** —*GARY*

In the early Seventies, we were on tour in Canada and I bought some smoke bombs. I had just replaced the pickups on my Les Paul with hand-wound DiMarizios—which [*Larry DiMarzio*] was winding in his bedroom at the time—and I wondered if the smoke would come out the pickup ring if a bomb was in the potentiometer. It worked, but it wasn't a great effect, and it badly gummed up my volume and tone controls. The idea manifested itself again when Kiss got bigger. I got together with an engineer and developed a fake rhythm pickup that snapped into a box mounted in the guitar's body. We stuck the smoke bombs in there, and it worked fine.

Sometimes, for a really big show, I'd have my tech pack in an extra-big bomb. When we did that, the metal plate on the guitar's back would heat up and burn my leg, or cause a little fire. When Paul [*Stanley*] and Gene [*Simmons*] sold a bunch of my costumes, I noticed that some of them had burn marks on the right leg.

Q: **Do you consider the classic solos in "Detroit Rock City" and "Love Gun" to be your best work?** —*BILL BETTIS*

Those two are obviously catchy and have been really popular, but I don't have any favorites. Some people freak out over the instrumentals like "Fractured Mirror." A friend says he put them all together on a CD and it works great for seducing women. Truthfully, though, once I've recorded something, I tend to move on and not look back.

Q: **How did you feel when Gene and Paul made you into everything from a comic-book hero to a condom style?** —*JAMES EDWARDS*

A lot of it was cool, and a lot of it was overkill, but it was out of my control, so I had to let it go. I left the group in '83 and didn't rejoin till '96, and during that time they took the ball and ran with it. Even when I rejoined, they made deals that I had no control over. I never saw the product until after the fact.

Q: **What effect are you using on the solo in "Strange Ways"? I love that sound.** —*ROY "SNAKE " HELVENSTINE JR.*

That was a heavy distortion unit—probably a Big Muff or a Fuzz Face—and a Marshall amp on 10. I usually performed my solos from the control room, with my amp out in the studio. But for "Strange Ways," I stood in front of the amp, which is how I got all the crazy feedback.

Did having to put makeup on every night ever get annoying?

—TRAVIS BOWLING

Yeah. Everything becomes a drag if you have to do it night in and night out. One of my worst experiences happened in Paris in the Seventies. I drank too much champagne after a big show and fell asleep with my makeup on. I had an allergic reaction and woke up with my eyes swollen shut. I thought I had gone blind and was terrified. Our manager brought over a doctor who gave me cortisone shots, and that fixed it.

Q: How long did it take you guys to put your makeup on each night?
—CHANCE HOWE

About an hour, sometimes a little longer, if we had the time. I could throw it on in half an hour if I had to, but the lines wouldn't be as straight.

Q: What do you like so much about the Les Paul? Have you ever played another guitar on an album or onstage? —MIKE WILLIAMSON

In the studio I've often doubled my parts with Fender Strats or Telecasters. The harmonic range of a Fender is different than that of a Les Paul, and you get a much thicker sound by blending them. I really like Fenders in the studio but I can't get the meat and sustain I want from them live. The Les Paul is the only guitar that I would consider a heavy rock guitar. It just has everything I want and need.

Q: In 1973, on the *Midnight Special* TV show, Kiss were playing "She" when you let loose with some crazy Van Halen–style two-handed tapping. This was, of course, long before "Eruption." How and when did you learn how to tap like that? —STEPHANIE

First, it obviously wasn't "Van Halen style." Gene discovered Van Halen, and I remember Eddie Van Halen sitting in the pit watching me tap at Madison Square Garden. I'm not saying Eddie got it from me, but I definitely didn't get it from him. I just picked that up over the years from experimentation. The one difference in how I tap is that I actually use my pick instead of my fingers.

Q: Which songs did you play on Kiss' *Psycho Circus* CD? The leads on "It's My Life" and "You Wanted the Best" sound like you, as does some of the toggle switching on "Journey of 1,000 Years." —G.S.

Uh, sure. That sounds right. [*laughs*] I honestly don't know which tracks I played on. I may have played on every track, for all I know. I wasn't there for all the sessions, and Tommy [*Thayer*] was around for some, but I couldn't tell you how it all shook out.

Q: Did you ever get tired of Gene's theatrics? —BAXTER HALL

Not really. Gene's theatrics are great and a trademark part of Kiss. We are a theatrical rock group, and as long as the fans want to see that, they are going to get it.

The only thing about Gene that sometimes gets overbearing is he'll try to come over

I just wanted to let you know that Kiss sucks without you.

—PAUL SANTOS

Thanks. Everyone's entitled to his opinion, and some people have said they think the group sounds better now. They must not have ever heard the original lineup, though.

to me when I'm playing and shove his tongue down my throat. He actually made it one time, and I had to run off stage and gargle with Listerine.

 Hey have you ever thought of forming a band with [*former Kiss drummer*] Peter Criss? —*MORGAN HARRIS*

Not really, but it could be cool. Usually when I got off the road from a Kiss tour, I tried to distance myself from all three guys because we get a little sick of each other. And I've always used [*drummer*] Anton Fig for my solo stuff.

 You have a great sound. What pickups do you use, and what is in your pedal board? —*VINCE APPLEGATE*

I don't have a pedal board because I trip over them with my boots on. I have a rack under the stage that my roadie controls. It has different gear in it at different times, although it always has an MXR graphic equalizer, a Big Muff and power booster. The last few tours I also had a Line 6 Pod. But the real key to my sound is that I always blend three sounds: usually my rackmount, my Marshall and another Marshall with a sealed cab and Celestion 12-inch speaker with a mic inside.

 Was it ever difficult to play in those costumes? They look uncomfortable. —*STEFFEN GOUZECKY*

Mine wasn't nearly as bad as Gene's. He's got all that armor, while mine was mostly spandex and stuff I could pop off and on. My boots, however, became a balancing act—and I'm pretty notorious for my bad balance. I used to fall a lot, and Paul and Gene would pretend it was part of the show.

DEAR GUITAR HERO

SLASH

The "Sweet Child O' Mine" riff mangles my fingers every time I try to learn it. Do you use some kind of secret technique? —*MATTHEW STEELE*

There's no secret technique. That's just my pick-up-a-guitar-and-fuck-around-with-it style of playing. That whole riff was just a mistake—a joke, really. To this day, I find it incredibly ironic and hilarious that it turned into a song, especially such a successful one. The riff started out as a stupid exercise that I noodled around with nearly every time I picked up a guitar. I don't really know how to practice properly, so I like to make up things that are difficult to play, so that I can become better at what I do.

Anyway, I must have played that riff a million times without ever thinking it would be a song. Then one day, while I was playing the riff, Izzy [*Stradlin, former Guns N' Roses guitarist*] started playing some chords, and the thing just took off! I think that just goes to show the value of doing things on the guitar that get you out of the box.

What was the hardest song you ever recorded, one that was just an absolute bitch to nail? —*ROBERT MCHUGH*

There are a few of them, including "Sweet Child O' Mine." That solo intro seemed impossible, even though I'd played the riff alone, without the band, for years. I almost never do more than two or three takes, but that one took at least eight. It was pretty frustrating.

I also had a really hard time nailing the intro solo on "Paradise City." It just wasn't "jamming" enough, as far as I was concerned. I finally had to quit for the day and go home, but I came back the next day and nailed it in one take. It was devastating to leave the studio with that song unfinished. I have a very short attention span.

The last song that comes to mind is a ballad on the Velvet Revolver record, "You Got No Right." We recorded it right after we wrote it. When I went to do the solo, it just didn't feel right, but I couldn't figure out why. We ended up rerecording the song a month or two later, and I nailed the solo right away. Before that, I'd never gotten into a rut where I couldn't play a solo because the whole feel was just off.

Who are some of your more obscure guitar inspirations? —*SHAWN HENRY*

I like the Pretenders' James Honeyman-Scott; the Cars' Elliot Easton, who is one of the best lead players of the last 25 years; Joe Walsh, who's one of the best rock and roll guitar players of all time; and the Sex Pistols' Steve Jones. I'm also a fan of Elvis Presley's guitarist Scotty Moore and [*surf-rock guitarist*] Dick Dale—to this day I haven't

had the balls to sit down and learn one of his songs. And I shouldn't forget David Lindley, who played with Jackson Browne for years. It might surprise some people to hear me say it, but the dude is incredible.

Q: **I can never seem to get that heavily accented wah sound that I closely associate with you and Kirk Hammett. Is your wah pedal tweaked?**
—*DAVID ZAMORA*

When I did *Appetite for Destruction* I had a stock Cry Baby. Now I own Dunlop wahs that are fully adjustable: you can decide where the wah starts and ends and make the high end sing longer or the low end more guttural. But to be honest, I don't use those features very much. Besides, you can definitely get a good wah sound without them. I think you should just keep experimenting. I'm sure whatever problem you're having has nothing to do with your pedal.

Q: **Is it true that you don't know scales?** —*MARCELO DUTRA*

Although I was never properly schooled in scales, over the years I've learned what a scale is and how to put together a series of notes that sound harmonically correct. But there are a lot of players whose technical knowledge is far superior to mine—guys that have a good grasp of music theory and apply it to their playing all the time. I can't do that, but I do know how to take a basic scale and change the notes around to suit my needs. I also know how to play major, minor and pentatonic scales all the way up the neck, but that's about as complicated as I get.

Q: **I have always admired your sound. Please list your setup.** —*JOHN VENTURA*

Thanks. People ask me this question all the time, and it's sort of funny. Because, to be honest, all you need is a decent-sounding Les Paul and a decent-sounding Marshall 100-watt or 50-watt head. That's it. The only other things I use are the occasional Boss EQ and wah pedal. I'd love to make it sound more interesting, but I'd be lying.

Q: **The solo on "Serial Killer," from the Slash's Snakepit album *Ain't Life Grand*, doesn't sound like anything you would play, with arpeggios and flat-out shredding instead of pentatonic phrases. Is that someone else playing, or is it a secret side of yourself that you've kept hidden? If so, you shouldn't do that. I consider "Serial Killer" to be a perfect song.** —*BRIAN INGOLD*

11

If you could record an album with one other guitarist, alive or dead, who would it be?

—BRANDON MOORE

I've played with Keith Richards and would love to take that further. And I would love to jam with Joe Walsh. But when I think of people I would love to jam with, I usually think of great rhythm sections rather than guitar players. Great lead guitar players usually don't need another lead player around. The multiple lead guitar sound of bands like the Allman Brothers and Lynyrd Skynyrd is cool, but it's a different, very structured kind of lead playing, and that's something I don't really strive for.

Thanks. That is definitely me. The riff just took on a life on its own, and the solo was more or less appropriated from it. I do a lot of things people wouldn't expect from me; the music sort of tells me to take a left turn here or there, and I go with it.

Q: **You look healthier now then ever before. Have you changed your lifestyle, and if so, has this affected your playing?** —*SAUL BAILEY*

I don't spend time chasing dealers around anymore. After a while that kind of lifestyle becomes a drag. For me, it became a burden and a pain in the ass rather than something that was fun and exciting, so I just stopped. As a result, I spend more time focused on guitar. I'm just very into my guitar and my music now, and I have more energy to devote to it.

Q: **Do you have an overwhelming desire to kick Axl in the nads?** —*DOM SEGRETTI*

At this point, anything that goes on between me and Axl is personal, and I'd rather leave it at that. Thanks.

DEAR GUITAR HERO

TONY
IOMMI

OF BLACK SABBATH

Q: From what I understand, Black Sabbath started as a blues band. Have you ever considered returning to your roots and recording a blues-oriented album, and who are some of your favorite blues performers?
—*BENOIT CHAMPAGNE*

I've always listened to blues records—anything from B.B. King to John Mayall—and I have considered making a bluesy jazz album. But I think that if I did I'd release it under my own steam, rather than with Sabbath.

Q: Why is the SG your guitar of choice? Have you ever recorded a Sabbath tune with another type of guitar? Which songs? —*NIK SIMON*

I love the SG; it's light and I can get to the top frets really easily. But I did play a Fender Strat when we recorded "Wicked World" for the first Sabbath album.

Q: Could you tell the story of how you lost the tips of your [*middle and ring*] fingers on your fretting hand? How did you overcome such an incredible handicap? —*JAMES WIORA*

I got them trapped in a machine when I worked in a factory. At that time, hospitals were less well equipped to deal with injuries such as mine, and there was little they could offer to help with my recovery. So I decided to construct my own fingertips. I melted down a plastic bottle, cut out a couple of pieces and filed them down to size. Then I covered them with leather to help them grip the strings better. It took a lot of time and patience to get it all worked out, but it paid off in the end.

Q: What do you think of the recent trend toward digital modeling amps? Do you dig them, or are you a tube man? —*DAVID KASMINSKY*

Logic make some pretty good digital amps, but I have to say that, yes, I'm a tube man.

Q: *Heaven and Hell* is my favorite Sabbath album. What was it like working with Ronnie James Dio, and could you offer a one-word description of each Sabbath singer? —*BOB BINKLEY*

Dio was a great man to play with, particularly when we first got together. He was extremely professional, and we made some great music together. It has been the same with all the Sabbath vocalists—they're all talented and fantastic to work with, but impossible to sum up in one word, particularly if I'm going to avoid swearing.

Rumor has it Geezer Butler once got into a fistfight with AC/DC's Malcolm Young. What's the story, and who won? My money's on Geezer.
—AARON

I wasn't present at the time, but yes, Geezer and Malcolm did have some sort of altercation in a hotel room. Our bands were on tour together, and the guys were both very drunk. An argument broke out and it got pretty heated. But since Geezer and Malcolm are still around to tell the tale, I don't think it came to anything too serious.

Q: **In the Seventies, when you and Geezer had similar moustaches, could Ozzy tell you apart? Also, what brand of razor do you prefer?**
—*GARY SALISBURY*

Yes, Ozzy could always tell us apart. Nowadays I use a Gillette razor.

Q: **What do you consider to be your strengths and weaknesses as a guitarist?** —*STARSSCREAM*

I think my main strength is that, musically speaking, I stick to what I believe in. I've obviously had difficulties with problems caused by the loss of my fingertips, but I feel that I've overcome most of them.

Q: **I'm the lucky owner of an original 1969 Laney Supergroup top [*the head used by Iommi on early Sabbath albums*]. Is there any chance of you and Laney reissuing this incredible amp?** —*BENJAMIN DE WAAL*

Laney actually makes an Iommi amp, the GH100TI. You can check it out at iommi.com, along with information on all the equipment I use. I'm also currently working with Laney to produce a second version of the amp.

Q: **Dude, you so awesome! And your first and last names rhyme! Will there ever be another Sabbath album with the original lineup?** —*ANIL RANA*

That's the $24 million question, isn't it? To be honest, it doesn't seem very likely at the moment. But in the words of a certain British spy film, never say never.

DEAR GUITAR HERO

ALEX
LIFESON

OF RUSH

What alternate chord voicings or exotic modes might you suggest to help me out of a rut? —*RICH GRECZI*

I'm not that fluid when it comes to scales and modes. I just pick up the guitar and play. It's all about exploration: just tune the guitar any way you want and start playing. Or better yet, don't play for a while. When I do that, my fingers may be rusty but I end up playing much more interesting things.

 How do you remember all the intricate parts of every song you guys play? —*DICKY*

We've been playing a lot of these songs for 30 years, so they're stuck in my memory. Even so, for the first few weeks of rehearsal, we tend to sound like a really, really bad Rush tribute band. But then the muscle memory brings it back.

 How does playing with a virtuoso drummer like Neil Peart affect your own playing? —*DOUG HESSONG*

Feeling those drums behind you is quite an amazing experience. There's so much activity in there, and when Neil shifts rhythm, you can sense it go to the front or back edge of the beat—it's that tight. If you play rhythmically as a guitarist, it's wonderful to have that going on behind you.

 Were you ever behind on your housework and forced to do your laundry in Geddy Lee's dryers onstage? —*DAVE PRESCOTT*

No.

 How did you develop from a fairly standard blues player into a completely unique stylist? For example, the solo in "Limelight" is almost impossible to categorize. —*JOHN WHITE*

Playing in a three-piece led me to take a broader approach to the musical space I occupy. My style became quite rich harmonically and melodically because I consciously tried to develop broad-sounding chords—the kind that are suspended, with lots of open strings ringing out—as a reaction to playing with Geddy and Neil, who take up a lot of space. I really consider myself more of a rhythm guitarist than a soloist, but "Limelight" is probably my favorite solo of any that I've done, because it is so fluid and emotional—and hard to categorize.

Any regrets about naming your band after a cheap teenage inhalant?

—TIM VOLK

The cheap teenage inhalant didn't exist when we named our band. I have no regrets about naming our group after a good feeling.

Q: As a Canadian, could you publicly apologize to America for letting Bryan Adams come here? —*JOEY BISHOP*

Bryan Adams might not be what I want to put on, but he's a pop singer with a great voice and great guitar tone. Plus, he's done more for Canada than Rush have, because he works all the time. I envy him for that. And now he's become a very successful photographer.

 Q: Regarding Rush's "kimono phase," do you have any regrets about going onstage wearing the equivalent of satin pajamas? —*CHARLZZ*

They sure were comfortable, and I thought they looked cool at the time. We're not the only ones who should be embarrassed by what we wore in the Seventies and Eighties.

 Q: Rush took a long break following the late-Nineties deaths of Neil's wife and daughter. Did it feel extra special to play together again? —*ROCHELLE PHILLIPS*

It felt amazing. We really didn't think we would ever do it again. At one point, things looked so bleak for Neil that it was unlikely it would ever be in his heart to play again. He went from playing every day to not touching his drums for more than four years. Getting back in the studio and seeing him rediscover his love for music was remarkable, and going back on the road was wonderful. Our first night back onstage was in Hartford, Connecticut. About 15 minutes into the show, Ged and I were by the kit, and we looked at each other and made a connection that was probably the most powerful moment in our career—it was just the realization that we had gone through this horrible experience and were still here. We didn't take a single night for granted; every show was a joy to play.

DAVE
MUSTAINE

Q: I'm having trouble learning the intro to "Hangar 18." Any secrets you could throw my way? —*DAN MACKINNON*

You're kidding, right? Learn [*Metallica's*] "The Call of Ktulu," then try again.

Q: When soloing, do you visualize positions and scales on the neck, or do you just let it rip? —*BUGSY PARKER*

I just let it rip. I found out what a pentatonic scale is when I started taking lessons a few years ago. My teacher asked where we should start and I said, "At the beginning." He said, "You're kidding, right?" and I told him that while I know what I'm doing, I have no idea what any of it is. That's when he told me that I play a lot of pentatonics. And that's probably because deep down inside I'm really a fast blues player.

Q: Any chance of you getting back together with Marty Friedman? —*BILLY PIZARRO*

We discussed it, but he was asking too many questions I didn't have answers for, so I just had to let it go. The alternative music revolution really distracted us as a band while we were making *Risk* [*1999*], especially Marty. Hopefully his head will get back to a place where we can play together again.

Q: Do you have a favorite Megadeth solo of all time? —*ANDREW*

I would have to say "Kick the Chair," though for years it would have been "Holy Wars."

Q: Has your experience with extraterrestrials affected your music? —*HAROLD MCCONNELL*

Nick [*Menza, former Megadeth drummer*] is the guy who believes in aliens. I think that's a bunch of crap.

Q: Out of all your guitar players, who do you think was the best? —*STEPHAN WHITE*

That's like asking "Who's your favorite kid?" Chris Poland had a great style, but he was very high maintenance. Jeff Young was a very technical player but really not Megadeth's style. Marty was a great player with a unique style that fit the band perfectly, but his heart changed and he wanted to pursue pop music. He's kind of

like Richard Chamberlain in the movie *Shogun*, where the character was obsessed with becoming a samurai; he moved to Japan and married a Japanese chick. Al Pitrelli was really great, too, though more in terms of learning other people's stuff. I'm not sure he could have come up with some of Marty's ideas, but he could execute them really well. I don't think he felt fully a part of the group. It's hard to go from being the leader of your own project to being second fiddle—and he actually had to become fourth fiddle.

Q: **Is the new metalcore scene just a thrash rip-off with a new name?**
—ANONYMOUS

I'm not familiar enough with any of it, so I can't say. I know who the big players are, but none of it has appealed to me enough to go buy a record. I still love to hear guitar players playing solos. The guitar is such an incredible instrument, and if you tune all your stuff down and use the guitar as a percussion instrument to go with cookie-monster vocals—dude, that ain't what a guitar is supposed to be used for, and you know it. You don't have to blaze, but you've got to solo. Someone like David Gilmour can say more in three or four notes than Yngwie can say in 100, but at least they're both speaking.

Q: **Have you ever considered recording a Christian metal CD?** *—VICKY HILL*

You have to define your terms. Some people think a Christian is a Holy Roller, and some think being a Christian means living a self-deprecating life on your knees. Would I make a Christian metal CD like P.O.D.? No, because that's not in me. But if it means taking the music that I make and changing the lyrics so that they speak about my change in lifestyles and beliefs, then yes, I would certainly do that.

Q: **Is it true you threw up all over Chris Poland's heroin in Miami?**
—BLAKE BELL

Yes. Well, not exactly "all over" it. He had hidden it in a closet, wrapped in a towel, and I puked all over the towel. And the sick thing is, he still used it.

Q: **Could you explain what your "spider crawl" technique is?**
—JONATHAN COSTIGAN

It's just an economical chord-shifting method that I came up with that doesn't require that you move your hands too much from one string to the other. For example, if you were playing a D chord with your first finger on the fifth fret on the A string and your

Do you find it interesting that many of your political songs and lyrics are more relevant today than they were 10 to 15 years ago?

—SCOTT FARR

Nope. I've used the Bible as a historical crystal ball and paid close attention to what's taking place in society. I'm very outspoken, sometimes to a fault, especially when it borders on getting myself in trouble for saying stuff people might think is anti-American. I love my country and I'm a patriot. I signed up for the draft when I was 18, and I would have served if called to.

DEAR GUITAR HERO

JEFF
BECK

third finger on the seventh fret on the D string, the spider chord would land on the sixth fret on the low E string and the 8th fret on the A string. I developed it because I made a lot of noise when shifting chords and had to figure out a new technique.

 How do you feel about today's trend of not playing guitar solos?
—*DAVE DLUTOWSKI*

It appalls me. If you have two guitar players and one of them doesn't solo, something is very wrong. Most guys who don't play solos *can't* play solos. I've heard that on Slipknot's new record they bust out the chops we've heard they always had, and I'm really glad for that, because we're bringing up a whole generation of kids who think all you have to do is detune, bang away and have your pants halfway down your ass. That doesn't make you a guitar player; it makes you a dork. Play that sucker, and don't be afraid to solo, no matter what it sounds like. Everybody has to start some place.

 Your songwriting stays fresh album after album in standard tuning, while others find the need to tune down to stay "heavy." What kind of practice routine helps you maintain that edge? —*JOSHUA AMOS*

I don't practice very much, because when I pick up a guitar, I write. I've always recorded every riff I wrote and kept everything I recorded. I'm very miserly with my writing. For instance, the first thing I wrote after I left Metallica was "Set the World Afire," and I waited until Megadeth's third album to record it, because that was when it fit in. I never toss out a good idea.

As far as staying fresh, if you keep copying other people, you're just an imitator, not an innovator. I don't listen to my peers' music, so I never have to stand trial for ripping anyone off. My biggest influences are all from classic rock, particularly Led Zeppelin and the Beatles. A lot of bands play the same chord progression over and over, just holding different chords for different beats, but it's basically the same damn song—and I think you know who I'm talking about. I don't want to act like I'm better than they are, but when it comes to my music, I'm always thinking, How is this different from anything I've done before? I'm my own worst critic, and I have a very stringent technique I use to hold myself accountable. You have to go out on a limb and take a chance. You need to change without copying what's hot at the moment—which nowadays would mean detuning and not playing any solos. Fuck that! My kids can play some of that stuff.

Q: **How did the idea evolve to record with a 64-piece orchestra on your 2010 album** *Emotion & Commotion*? —ALBERT SHOROFSKY

I was listening to an interview that I did way back in 1966 with Brian Matthews, the guy that ran the *Saturday Club* radio show in England, and there was a clip where he asked me, "What would you like to see yourself doing in the future?" and I said, "I'd like to play with a big orchestra." [*laughs*] I couldn't believe that, even way back then, I was thinking about doing that. At the time, I'd seen Tina Turner and heard the amazing sounds of the Phil Spector productions that featured big, powerful string sections, and the orchestral sounds on other pop records, too. I thought, There couldn't be a better backdrop for some kind of powerful music than a big orchestra. My wish to hear how a guitar would sound in front of an orchestra has always been there.

I originally wanted to present two CDs in the box, with *Emotion*, the orchestral stuff, on one disc and *Commotion*, the stuff with the band, on the other. I went into the studio one day and [*producer*] Steve Lipson had sequenced the orchestral and band tracks together. He said, "What do you reckon?" and I said, "It sounds all right to me. Let's carry on!" Every time I walked into the studio, I wouldn't remember what I'd done the previous day, and there was no kind of rhyme or reason to what was going on until he started to sequence some of the demos together. We *forced* it together. The ingredients were pleasing musical pieces but there was no preconception to it, and it just happened.

Q: **In the mid Sixties, John Mayall's Bluesbreakers was a band that served as a training ground for some of Britain's best blues guitarists, such as Eric Clapton, Peter Green and Mick Taylor. Did Mayall ever ask you to join the Bluesbreakers?** —ALEX DURANT

He did. John called my mum several times. He found my mum's number, and she said to me, "Oh, that John Mayall sounds very nice!" [*laughs*] But I didn't want that—I didn't want to be playing blues all of the time. I'd seen Eric with them, and he was fantastic, really. He did the job better than I could have, and I just didn't want to have that challenge. My musical taste was changing radically from 12-bar blues. I might have done better in that band than in the Yardbirds, but I certainly would not have been given the same kind of free reign to do the experimenting that I did in the Yardbirds.

John Mayall came to see me with the Yardbirds at some gig. He was very straightforward.

He never embellished or gave us any flowery comments about the gig. He said, "The audience loved it, but there was not much *blues*, was there?" And I thought, Excuse me, but this isn't a blues band. It sort of was, but he's a purist and he was listening for Little Walter–style harmonica solos. I didn't want to be mimicking Chicago blues musicians forever. My thinking was, We're not them, we're not black, we're British middle-class kids and let's get on and do our own music. We had a bit of disharmony about that, but not to take away from John's dedication to it.

Q: **I've read about Jimi Hendrix coming every night for a week to jam with the Jeff Beck Group at the Scene Club in New York City. Can you describe what that was like and your relationship with Jimi?** —*CHARLES PIZER*
We did six nights in a row there [*in June 1968*]. The initial gig that broke us in America was at the Fillmore East with the Grateful Dead. But after that success and the great write ups, we then had to go down-market at a small club for six nights. It gave every-one a chance to watch what they had just seen again, six times in a row. We didn't really want to be scrutinized like that, in case we just happened to get lucky the night we played the Fillmore, which was quite good.

The first night at the Scene, Jimi didn't show up, but he came for the rest of the five nights. Around about the halfway mark, he'd come in from whatever recording he'd been doing. The buzz was incredible: the place was packed anyway, but when he came in they were standing on each other's shoulders. Sometimes he didn't have his guitar, so he would turn one of my spare guitars upside down and played that way, and I actu-ally played bass at one point. I've got a photograph of that. Thank god someone took a picture, because there's hardly any record of those goings-on.

Around that time, Jimi and I played a secret gig, a benefit at [*drug rehabilitation center*] Daytop Village. Jimi drove me up in his Corvette...that was the best mo-ment. His driving was terrible. We were stuck in traffic in the middle of New York City, and he had this brand-new 427 Corvette boiling over, and I thought, I hope it doesn't blow up right here! [*laughs*] I was thinking, Why did you buy a Corvette in Manhattan?

I wasn't looking for compliments, but before I met Jimi someone told me that he knew all about my recordings with the Yardbirds. He had to, because for someone so utterly flamboyant and played so inventively, I knew he was one for listening out. He wasn't one of those staid, insular kinds of blues players; he would listen to everything. And that alone thrilled me. He'd also seen the Yardbirds live in 1965/1966 when he was playing sideman to Little Richard, I believe. It was amazing to see him play, and I'd met him before I saw him perform. I saw him at this tiny little club in London, with all of these "dolly birds," which is what they called girls dressed in their miniskirts. I think they all thought he was going to be a folky, Bob Dylan–type of character [*laughs*], and he blew the place apart with his version of [*Dylan's*] "Like a Rolling Stone."

I just went, "Ah...this is so great!" It overshadowed any feelings of inferiority or competetiveness. It was so amazing. To see someone doing what I wanted to do... I came out a little crestfallen, but on the positive side, here was this guy opening big doors for us. Instead of looking on the negative side and saying, "We're finished," I was thinking, No, we've just started! I was delighted to have known him for the short time that I did. It was the magical watering hole of the Speakeasy, the club where we hung out in London, that enabled that to happen. It was the one place you could go and be guaranteed to see Eric or Jimi and have fun playing. Those places don't seem to exist anymore.

Q: There were so many incredible guitar players in England in the mid Sixties—you, Eric Clapton, Jimmy Page, Mick Taylor, Peter Green. Were each of you very aware of one another's careers? —*HUGH FINSECKER*

Mentally, there was some subliminal connection between all of us, wondering what one another were doing, but physically, no, we were not around each other very often at all. Eric lived not very far away from me at the time, and Jimmy lived not very far away, either, but I hardly ever saw Jimmy until I got him into the Yardbirds as the bass player.

I joined the Yardbirds in February of '65, and I'd never saw sight or sound or Eric with them before that. My only connection to him was hearing the rest of the band talking about him, that he used to do this, that and the other. I got pretty pissed off with it, like, "Shut up, I'm here now!"

I didn't see him untill about a year later, because we were off to America. Right when I joined the Yardbirds, they had a massive hit with "For Your Love," which Eric detested and was the reason he left the band. So we were off pummeling around the States on the three-week promo tour. When we went back [*to England*], by pure chance I bumped into him in a club and I thought we were actually going to get into a fight! But when he saw me, he went, "Hello, man!" and he gave me a big hug, and that was the end of that.

You've always played with a wonderful type of aggression, throwing wild sounds at the audience in a way that says, "Deal with this!" Where does that attitude come from?
—ANGELO BARTH

It's like a tantrum. Those things are outbursts, like exactly what I wanted to do to the teachers at school. It's a bottled-up frustration that manifests itself in those outbursts, as well as a reflection of my life and my reaction to the difficulties of it. Singers are like that when they start screaming, like Screaming Jay Hawkins [*Beck covers Hawkins' "I Put a Spell on You" on* Emotion & Commotion]: One minute he's singing perfectly normally, and then all of a sudden he bursts into rage. Love it.

I like an element of chaos in music. That feeling is the best thing ever, as long as you don't have too much of it. It's got to be in balance. I just saw Cirque du Soeil, and it struck me as complete organized chaos. And then there was this simple movement in the middle of the show, which was a comedy, and I thought, What a great parallel between the way that I think and the way this circus is happening. It had a special meaning for me, aside from the spectacle of it all. When I came away from it, I thought, If I could turn *that* into music, it's not far away from what my ultimate goal would be, which is to delight people with chaos and beauty at the same time.

BILLY F GIBBONS

OF ZZ TOP

Q: **Why did you start using a peso as a pick?** —*PAUL SHUFFIELD, JR.*

Tommy Carter of Jimmie Vaughan's Dallas band the Chessmen used a quarter to play bass. He described the serrated edge of the coin as producing a delightful scratchiness as he scrubbed the strings. That gave me the idea, and our love of the Mexican border is what drew us to the peso. The peso coin is a rarity, but we've still got a few filed down for the ready.

Q: **Does the fur affect your beloved tone?** —*CHRIS TRACY*

The fur on the guitar or my face?

Q: **You use six Bixonic Expandora pedals for distortion, which would seem to create a muddy mess. Do you set the levels differently on each one to create the desired sustain while maintaining a cleaner distortion sound? Please help. Not knowing makes my medication less effective.** —*KEVIN POTTS*

You are correct. Combinations of multiple effects are manageable when using a slight edge from each, which avoids the unwanted collision of tones. However, at this point, sometimes the grind of excessive noise becomes its own thing! Experiment...just not with your medication.

Q: **Do you really use .008 gauge strings? If so, how do you keep them from flapping when detuning? And how do you get such a great tone, since I have always believed the bigger the strings, the better the tone?**
—*BRIAN WACHTER*

I, too, once believed in the heavier gauge string as a superior tone source. However, thanks to the graciousness of B.B. King I learned that a lighter gauge string offers superior playing comfort. Detuning requires some adjustment of attack, approach and feel. Try it. You may like it.

Q: **Please tell me about your fantastic-sounding Pearly Gates. Was it love at first sight, and how and why does it sound so damn good?**
—*PETER OHMER*

She is a 1959, and I acquired her when I was 18. While I have always been in love with her, I would have to say it was *luck*, not love, at first sight. We've studied the varying construction techniques used on a wide range of Les Pauls, and Pearly Gates seems

simply to have been on the assembly line on the right day at the right time. It was the right glue, the right wood, the right finish on the right day. It's just all good.

Where can I get one of those pimp-ass hats? —*GAREN HENRY*

From a Bamileke tribal member in Cameroon, West Africa. Be sure to take a Texas 10-gallon along for good trading.

Did Frank play drums on *Eliminator* and did you play any guitar synth on the album? —*AC JOHNSON*

Frank played his trusty acoustic kit and used triggers to activate sounds on his drum modules. Although a guitar synth was present, we focused our attention on one of Mr. Moog's keyboard contraptions.

Ever jam with Johnny Winter when you were both young Texas bucks? —*MICHAEL MOSLEY*

I was fortunate enough to join the legion of Johnny Winter fans when he first launched the great Johnny Winter trio [*with bassist Tommy Shannon and drummer Uncle John Turner*]. We were content to remain in awe and admiration without attempting to crowd the stage.

You are the king of artificial harmonics. How do you hit them so smoothly and exactly? —*MATT BUSH*

Quite simply: it's meat on metal on wood. Roll the picking fingers slightly off edge of the plectrum and move around a bit. The sound changes drastically and requires some experimentation until you get comfortable finding your sweet spots.

You are well known for your pinch harmonics. What boggles my mind is how you do harmony between the pitches on the same fret. I'm think-ing of "La Grange." How do you know each note's pitch and harmonize them perfectly? —*JOSH BERRY*

See the answer to the question above. It's a tricky thing to do, until muscle memory becomes second nature. Striking exactly where you want to requires some guesswork, especially while you are learning the technique. Again, experiment until you're playing what you want to hear.

I apologize if my question causes you nightmares, but if you had to choose between blowing up all of your custom hot rods and chopping up all of your guitars and amps with an ax, which would you do?
—DALLAS TRINGALI

Oh my God! We'd probably prefer to take a quick cruise and play each guitar, and burn the whole *house* down!

I love the way it sounds like two guitar players dueling back and forth on *Deguello* and would like to confirm what I know but still find hard to grasp: that is all you, right? —*RUSSELL D LANCASTER*

Correct. The magic of multitracking turned our trio into a multipiece combo. Having to do it all simply requires the virtue of patience.

You had a keyboard player on the first ZZ album. How did the group decide to become a three-piece? What are your likes and dislikes about playing in a trio? —*BRIAN BIRCKBICHLER*

Our first recording *did* feature ZZ top as a trio, but instead of using guitar, drums and bass, we used guitar, drums and a Hammond B-3 organ. [*ZZ Top's first single, "Salt Lick" b/w "Miller's Farm," features this lineup. The tracks are available on the* Chrome, Smoke & BBQ *box set (Rhino)*]. The power of the kick [*bass*] pedals from the keyboard allowed us to create a four-piece sound with the minimalism of a trio, which is what we have always loved. Presently, ZZ Top enjoys the challenge that trio performance requires. Quite lively.

You enjoyed the privilege of hanging out with many esteemed bluesmen that have since passed away. What was the most valuable wisdom you picked up from one of these legends? —*FRANCINE BYRD*

Two pieces of advice come to mind: Lightnin' Hopkins taught us, "The rubber on a wheel is faster than the rubber on a heel." And Muddy Waters taught us, "You don't have to be the best one; just be a good 'un." That just about says it all. Always strive to be a good 'un!

 Have you always been a sharp-dressed man? I saw some old photos of you guys in cheesy blue cowboy suits, which stopped me in my tracks. —*RYAN JONES*

To borrow Dusty's expression, we're immune to fashion. Thank goodness for the notion that accompanies the vision of sharp-dressed men. We're still trying to figure that one out.

You have always had fabulous tone. What amps and guitars did you use on ZZ Top's first few albums? —*RICK PAULUS*

Thanks very much. We have been fortunate to enjoy the luxury of a spot-on crew, and we've maintained an archive of each instrument, amp, drum kit and ancillary devices

Did you really fall out of your chair when you first saw Shawn Lane play guitar?

—RUDY BOLNER

Yes. And no Mexican cerveza was involved. Shawn still holds dear to all of us who were able to witness his six-string prowess. He was a remarkable musician.

used on each track. It's all on record, and any piece of gear can be lifted from the vault for most particular sounds. At the heart of almost everything we've done, however, is Pearly Gates run through either a Marshall or an old Fender. That simple-but-deadly combination is still tough to beat.

Q: **Is it true that you bought 100 Smokey guitar amps [*tiny amps contained in cigarette cases; visit smokeyamps.com for more info*], and if so, have you ever used one on an album?** —*JEFF HUCLE*

Ha-ha! Yes, we did make the purchase, and you'll probably hear these little devils in some form on the upcoming Top release. We have not had the opportunity to put them to use in the studio as of yet.

Q: **Whose idea was it to build a stage in the shape of your home state on the Worldwide Texas Tour?** —*KAMIL Z.*

That inspired idea was the result of a bragadocious band meeting a big-time production house. Ideas kept getting bigger and more bodacious, and then we had to figure out how to pull it all off.

Q: **You're known for your fine taste in vintage and custom guitars and for amassing a massive collection thereof. But tell us about the elusive one that got away.** —*ALAN PARTRIDGE*

There are too many to choose from. Just when you think you've seen it all, up jumps the mystery piece and the chase starts all over again. I would like to note that, right now, there is a Gretsch in production based on a guitar originally gifted to Bo Diddley in 1959. It's good, so don't let it get away.

JIMMY PAGE

Q: **Would you ever accept a knighthood?** —*MS. AMANI REDD*

I'm never going to be offered one, so it doesn't really cross my mind. [*laughs*] But I would think long and hard about it. I know a lot of people who would say, "Forget about that," but it's something you would have to seriously consider.

Q: **Is part of "The Crunge," from *Houses of the Holy*, in a different tuning?** —*JOHN B. BLACK*

No, it's all in standard tuning. It was all played pretty much in a single take.

Q: **Your black dragon stage outfit from the mid Seventies was awesome. Where did it come from?** —*RACHEL BOCKOVER*

It was made by a woman from L.A. named Coco. I basically outlined what I wanted on it. For example, I asked her to personalize the pants with astrological symbols—Capricorn, Scorpio rising, Cancer.

I still have that suit, and the amazing thing about it is that it still looks brand new, like it just came off the peg. I did a lot of roadwork in that thing and it's in wonderful condition. Most of my other clothes ended up in tatters, but the dragon suit still looks great.

I thought about want I wanted on my stage clothes carefully. After Coco made the dragon outfit, I had her make my white suit with the poppy on it. I would wear the black dragon one night and the poppy suit the next. It became a ritual for me.

Q: **Have you ever gone into a music store and played "Stairway to Heaven"?** —*CARY SALISBURY*

No, I haven't. [*laughs*]

Q: **How did you come up with the idea of using a violin bow on the guitar on songs like "Dazed and Confused"?** —*NICK OLSON*

While I was playing studio sessions in the days before Led Zeppelin, I would often play with string sections. For the most part, the string players would keep to themselves, except for a guy who one day asked me if I ever thought of playing my guitar with a bow. I said I didn't think it would work because the bridge of the guitar isn't arched like it is on a violin or cello. But he insisted that I give it a try, and he gave me his bow. And whatever squeaks I made sort of intrigued me. I didn't really start developing the technique for quite some time later, but he was the guy that turned me onto the idea.

When do you think Led Zeppelin peaked?

—MATT JAGEL

Hmm. I don't know how to answer that. I don't think the band ever peaked. I always felt we were at our finest hour. It never really got stale. I mean, *Presence* gets overlooked, but I love the intensity of that album. It's full on. We recorded it while Robert was recovering from a terrible car accident. He was in a wheelchair and we were uncertain that he would ever walk again. That urgency came across in every song. We recorded it in about two weeks, and whoever got up first would just start working to get it done. It required a sort of keen energy that I'm not sure I have anymore.

Q: **Have you ever thought about designing a tarot deck?** —*DAN HOVER*

No. It would take a long, long time to do. The Aleister Crowley deck took ages for him to design. I'm having a hard enough time finding a moment to focus on music. It's been a really busy time for me. I spent close to three years working on *Led Zeppelin DVD* and *How the West Was Won*, and then I moved home with my family and my children, which was very time consuming. But things are starting to settle down.

Q: **In the early days of rock and roll, everybody played the guitar at armpit level. Then you came along and started playing it slung low. Was it about image or was it more comfortable for you to play it low?** —*WES CARTER*

You have to understand, while I was in Led Zeppelin I was living and breathing it. It became a lifestyle, including wearing my guitar low, gunslinger style. Rock musicians at the time were like outlaws, and as in the movies, our holsters just got lower and lower.

Q: **Did playing with Bonzo for 12 years make it hard for you to play with other drummers?** —*NICK HUGHES*

Well, having John Bonham playing drums for you, as well as having Robert Plant sing and John Paul Jones play bass, gave me confidence to know that anything I would write would come out good in the end.

Q: **Your tone on "Whole Lotta Love" slays me every time. What were you playing through?** —*MIKE*

I think I played the main riff through a Vox Super Beatle.

YNGWIE
MALMSTEEN

Q: I am from Mumbai City, India. You have a huge fan base here, and I would like to know if you ever plan to tour India. We have huge respect for Indian-classical maestros, and would love to see a legend like you collaborate with some of them. —*KHUSHAL BHADRA*

I'd love to perform in India, but I don't book the gigs. It's one of the few places I haven't played. One of the Indian instruments that I love is the sitar. I played it on some of my songs, including "Pyramid of Cheops" and "Crucify." The sitar is a bizarre instrument, because it has a very big neck and no wood in between the frets—the ultimate scalloped instrument. I love all kinds of Indian music, and Indian food as well. If the chance arises for me to play in India, I'm there.

Q: How, and at what age, did you come across sweep picking? —*ANDY CLARK*

I don't really do sweep picking. That's a big misconception people have about my playing. Sweep picking is when the right hand sweeps down and up the strings in succession. But when you do sweep picking, one note rings into the next, and it sounds almost like you're playing a chord, and that's exactly what you don't want. Playing five- and six-string arpeggios the way I do, like on "Caprici De Diablo," for instance, you want separated notes that don't go into one other. People that try to play my stuff often do sweep picking, but the results are usually pretty dismal.

Q: In the first of the Pantera home videos, Dimebag Darrell offered you a doughnut, which you didn't accept. What food would you have accepted from Dime? And what's your problem with doughnuts? *JOACHIM ARNT*

I've never seen that clip, but I've been asked that question before. First of all, I don't remember that incident. Second, I don't make a habit of accepting food from people. I'm fortunate enough not to have to do that because I can buy my own food.

Q: Can you tell me your strategies to build speed and improve fret-hand abilities? —*JUAN FRANCISCO PURDON*

I don't have any "strategies." What I've done from the very beginning is play everything with extreme accuracy. I never said to myself, "Okay, if I put my fingers this way, it's gonna result in this." I've never taken a lesson. My way of playing the guitar was a fresh approach to the instrument. There's no specific technique to what I do, except for the fact that you have to coordinate your picking and your fingering so they are perfectly

What made you want to cover Michael Jackson's "Beat It" on your 2009 album *High Impact*? Were you a fan of his, or were you paying tribute because he died?

—TEDDY OPERAND

It was a tribute to him, but I've always liked the song. It's my heavy metal version of the song, with detuned guitars and Ripper Owens on vocals. Unlike the original, I begin with a guitar solo, and there's another solo in the middle of the track. It's not too much like the original. I played it my own way, like I did on my *Inspiration* album, where I covered songs from other artists.

in sync, but that's obvious. You can't "build" speed; you play it until you have it perfect. There are no shortcuts and no tricks. The saying "practice makes perfect" is truthful. Sometimes people try to play too fast and it sounds sloppy. I can't stand that.

 How do you manage to keep your Strat in tune when you're constantly doing huge dive bombs and pull-ups? —*MICHAEL MCLAUGHLIN*

I couldn't tell you exactly how I keep my guitar in tune, but I think it's how I tune it. The strings are wound on the pegs exactly right. If you have too few windings, the string might slip; if you wind it too much, the string might not pull back properly after you use the whammy. Basically, you have to find just the right amount of winding. I beat the shit out of my guitars onstage, but they stay perfectly in tune.

Besides guitar playing, what other things do you like to do? —*JEFF HERNANDEZ*

I love driving my Ferraris, hanging out with my family, going to the movies, reading books and messing with my watches. I'm also a tennis freak and play as much as I can. Tennis is like chess and boxing combined into one. It's not a team sport—it's all about *you*. It's very intelligent, psychological and physical. You have to be smart to play it, because you need to quickly anticipate your opponent's move. It's quite a mental challenge and also very humbling. My tennis coach is the only guy who has ever taught me anything in my life. Whatever he says goes.

Why don't you try to reinvent your style? Ninety nine percent of people I know who like your music say, "Yngwie makes the same record over and over again." Is it time to take the neoclassical style to the next level? —*RAUL GOMEZ*

Raul, have you ever heard of Eric Clapton? He's been playing the same five notes for 50 years! B.B. King has been playing the same three notes for 60 years! The Rolling Stones have been playing the same chords for 50 years! The kind of music that I make is quite diverse in the sense that it doesn't just have one aspect—it goes from neoclassical to bluesy to metal. People who think that I make the same record over and over again are narrow-minded.

Any artist who has their own sound, from Sting to Iron Maiden to ZZ Top—for them to change would be mad. Having your own definable sound is something that should

How do you respond to the people that accuse you of being arrogant?

—CHRIS

I tell them to fuck off! I saw an old interview with Queen on TV recently, and Freddie Mercury and Brian May were talking about how they were when they started: arrogant, cocky and convinced they'd conquer the world. You have to be like that if you're really gonna make it. If you're timid, laid-back and quiet, you have less chance of being noticed. So maybe there was an arrogant side to me when I started out. You have to be cutthroat and go for it all the way. Obviously, I don't have a need for that anymore. I just do what I do.

be treasured. Nobody tells Angus Young to change. Anyone who has a narrow-minded view of me, well, what do *they* have to offer? I'm proud to have started a style of music that has been copied. How could someone ask me to reinvent my style? What kind of talk is that? I'm an artist. I'm not a waiter who takes orders from people. As for taking my neoclassical style to the next level, I composed a symphony [Concerto Suite for the Electric Guitar and Orchestra, 1998]. How's *that* for the next level!

 Not to take anything away from your creativity and technical skill, but why are there so many similarities between you and Ritchie Blackmore: scalloped fretboard, Fender Strat, Marshall amps, black clothing?
—*DOUG NEWMAN*

When I was eight, my sister gave me my first record—Deep Purple's *Fireball*. Blackmore's playing on that album affected me greatly and had a major impact on my life. Obviously, I wanted a Strat, and when I first started playing one I realized it was the perfect instrument—the Stradivarius of electric guitars. The Marshall amp is the best-sounding, best-looking amp, and there will never be anything better. I like black clothes because they look good, and I like scalloped fretboards because they allow you to have better control of the vibrato.

But musically, I really don't have all that much in common with Blackmore; much of his guitar playing is blues based, whereas mine is more classical. Anyone who'd claim that my guitar playing and style of music is similar to Blackmore's is tone deaf.

DEAR GUITAR HERO

BOB
WEIR

Q: One thing that makes your rhythm style so unique is you usually play licks rather than chords. Are you actually a lead guitarist in hiding?
—*RYAN GRAY*

I consider myself a structural guitarist. I'm consumed with a song's architecture, the arc of the groove and the movement from passage to passage. I try to get in between the bass, drums and keyboards and be very selective about what I play—rarely more than two notes in any chord. A keyboard player can play 10 notes, and when you add that to two guitars and a bass the sound can become too thick. Rather than be a part of that problem, I try to align myself with something else, often the keyboard player's left hand, perhaps supplying a few extra notes to his chord. What I'm doing is usually dependent on what somebody else is doing.

Q: When was the last time you took LSD? —*DANK BUD*

Many, many years ago. I believe the last time I willingly took it was July 31, 1966. There was nothing more to be gained, but there were some accidental dosings.

Q: I recently heard you play the acoustic part on "Ripple" and wondered how it feels to play Jerry Garcia's parts. —*DANIEL JOHN WILSON*

I prefer not to play Jerry's parts simply because it means I have to abandon my own old parts. That said, it's a lot of fun and it expands my knowledge, because playing a part once can provide insight, even into something you've heard 1,000 times. Any band could benefit from having its members swap parts once in a while.

Q: Why do you always wear shorts onstage? Do you own any pants?
—*SCOTT JONES*

I do own pants, but I get hot easily and it gets to me. It's always July under the lights, so I wear shorts and workout shirts onstage. The whole deal is I want to keep cool.

Q: You play a lot of lead-like riffs. Did you come up with complementary parts on songs like "China Cat Sunflower" in response to what Jerry played, or vice versa? —*JON COMAY*

I always played a lot of counterpoint in support of Jerry's guitar or vocal melody. "China Cat Sunflower" is an odd example because it's virtually the only song on which Jerry taught me a riff and told me it's what he wanted to hear. That little arpeggiated lick

Supposedly, the other members of the Grateful Dead hatched a plot to fire you and Pigpen in 1968. Did you know that was going on? How was that tension resolved?

—DOUG GRANEY

They actually did fire us, but I won't go into details. The group went on without us for a few months and it didn't work, so we got asked back. The tensions resolved themselves; you have to let bygones be bygones. It was all part of growing up. I was maybe 20 years old at the time.

was his. I do something similar on "Scarlet Begonias," a part that I came up with. The concept of the band was always group improvisation, not merely playing behind Jerry's solos. The Grateful Dead's m.o. was to play rock in the style of Dixieland jazz, where every instrument plays a crucial role in support of one another.

 Is it true that you hate tie-dyes? —*TIM PENN*
Yep. They just never appealed to me.

 Through the early Eighties, the simpler tone you got with your Gibson 335 allowed your immaculate choice of chord inversions to shine through the mix. Do you still own that old 335, and is there any chance you'll go back to it? —*GIN KANEKO*

It's one of my favorite guitars and I bust it out every now and then, but it's become too valuable to take out on the road regularly. Plus, I've become too entrenched in single-coil pickups to return to that big, fat sound. Frankly, I don't think it was the guitar that allowed you to hear my playing more back then. Prior to the time you refer to, our sound mixer was delusional and certainly taking a lot of drugs. He thought he should have my gig, so he mixed me way down until I finally had to get him fired.

Describe your approach to using arpeggiated or substituted chords behind Jerry's solos on songs like "Playing in the Band" or "Dark Star." —*KYLE MILLER*

What you do is listen to the other guy intently and try to intuit where he's going, then get there first with something that's either complementary or an interesting juxtaposition. If I knew where Jerry was going to finish a phrase, I could be waiting with either something that was tonic and would push him in that direction or something that put a leading tone on top of his last phrase and would spur the music in a different direction. It's a lot of fun. Our group communication in both the Dead and Ratdog is now reaching the level where such things are possible.

BRIAN
SETZER

Q: **Which classic rockabilly artists would you recommend I check out to better understand the style?** —*JIMMY VOMVAS*

The definitive rockabilly album for me was Elvis Presley's *The Sun Sessions*. Boy, oh boy. That probably has everything you need all wrapped up right there. Also pick up the first two Gene Vincent records: *Blue Jean Bop* and *Gene Vincent and the Blue Caps*. As a guitar player, you have to hear Cliff Gallup play with Gene Vincent and Scotty Moore play with Elvis Presley.

Q: **Your playing style is so incredible and immaculate. Did you start with any jazz guitar training or did you just learn how to play "Stairway to Heaven" like the rest of us?** —*JON RUBIN*

[*laughs*] I'm not saying I didn't play it. Hell, we *all* played it; it's a classic. But I did take guitar lessons for about 10 to 12 years, with two different teachers. I took my first lesson when I was eight years old. I went through the Mel Bay books. Back then in Long Island, New York, there were mostly jazz players. So my first teacher was actually a saxophone player. After that I studied with this other jazz teacher, Ray Gogarty. He took me further into the jazz world: advanced chords, a little bit of the modes, scales and standards.

Q: **What attracted you to using Gretsch hollowbodies as your main guitars?** —*JEFF OSGOOD*

The first reason I wanted to play a Gretsch guitar is because Eddie Cochran played one. Believe me, when I was growing up, nobody knew who he was. I just stumbled across this record and I thought he looked cool. I had no idea he was that good. But once I popped on the record, it was exactly the guitar sound that I wanted: somewhere between a Fender and Gibson. To me, if you play a Fender straight through the amp without any effects, it's a little thin sounding. And a Les Paul didn't twang enough; it was just always on 11, you know? The Gretsch was right between those two. It had that twang, but you could really make it sing if you wanted. I guess it just fulfilled the sound I was hearing in my head.

Q: **I seem to remember reading that one of the cars on Stray Cats' *Built for Speed* album cover was yours. Is that true?** —*ERIC SMOOT*

Yeah, the '56 Chevy on the cover of *Built for Speed* was mine. That Chevy actually got

What first inspired you to play guitar?

—MOLLY MCALLISTER

I was a little kid, like six or seven years old, when the Beatles came out. I remember hearing their music and I couldn't imagine where that sound was coming from. Then I saw a picture of the Beatles, and George [*Harrison*] had an electric guitar, and I was like "That's it!" It was that sound—the sound of George's guitar—that first captured me when I was really young. It all goes back to that sound.

stolen from a parking spot years ago. I wish I still had it. I came back from doing what I was doing, and the car was gone. It broke my heart.

Q: **What led you down the rockabilly path?** —*STEVE*

The real defining moment for me was when I heard [*Gene Vincent's*] "Be-Bop-A-Lula" on the jukebox. Back in 1976 or '77, we had this club in Manhattan called Max's Kansas City. There was always punk music blasting, but for some reason one day "Be-Bop-A-Lula" came on the jukebox. It was as if a hand came across the bar and grabbed me, like, "Listen to me! Listen to how cool I am!" There was just something about the raw, back-to-basics sound that fit perfectly with the urgency of the punk movement I was in back then. To me, rockabilly music paralleled punk's energy and feeling, but the players were *much* better. I'm telling you, I still remember Cliff Gallop's solo coming out of the speaker. I went, "What the heck is that? Who's playing this?"

Q: **I know you co-wrote some tracks with [*late Clash singer and guitarist*] Joe Strummer for your *Guitar Slinger* album, and I heard that you were friends with him, as well. Can you share any good stories?** —*COLE SLAUGH*

Oh, I've got a *lot* of great memories with Joe. Joe and I would spend the summers together because we were good friends and we both had children. So we'd throw the kids in the pool and have a good time. Joe had a very good, dry sense of humor, you know, and some of the things he would say were just... Well, let's say he was very good at making fun and making light of a situation. If you were wound up or you were aggravated about something, Joe would say a couple words, and then you would laugh and realize how silly the whole thing was. He was a great guy, and a genius of our time.

Q: **I love your live sound. But I'd like to know how you control feedback at stage volume. I have had this issue with hollowbody guitars in the past.** —*ERIC A. NAY*

I've actually never had any problems with the [*Gretsch*] 6120 with FilterTron pickups. The feedback that I get is kind of friendly feedback. It's like a note, not a squeal. I love what happens on a hollowbody guitar when you're too close to an amp. That sound comes back through the guitar and vibrates the body, like an old jalopy or something. That's the most magical feeling to me. Once you figure it out, you can kind of control all of those feedback notes.

I really dig your hair. What is your secret ingredient? Are you a Murray's Pomade man?

—JOE BARRIOS

[*in a radio-announcer voice*] You've heard of Dapper Dan? Well, I'm a Murray's man! [*laughs*] As my dad used to say, "You've got to train your hair." And then once you've got it trained, you comb it in the position, throw in a little bit of Murray's…and you'll be a Murray's man, too. [*laughs*]

You've got an amazing sound. What is your main amp-and-effect setup?
—*BILLY WILSON*

I just use a '63 Fender Bassman and a Roland Space Echo. I mean, my amps have been worked on, but they're not modified—rather de-modified. Over the years people have put in the wrong tubes, cables and speakers. I try to get the Bassmans back to stock, and I like to use Celestion Vintage 30s for the speakers. I think they're better matched to the power of the amplifier head.

 I've always been impressed by your right-hand picking technique. Could you give me any advice on how to refine mine? —*GREG TERZIAN*

Well, first of all, anyone that tells you "This is the only right way to do it" is wrong. Any way you feel comfortable fingerpicking…if it works for you, then do it. There's not a wrong or a right way. When I fingerpick, I tuck my pick under my index finger; I'll slip it down when I use the guitar pick, and then I tuck it up, and use my thumb, second, third and fourth fingers to fingerpick. I've never heard of anyone doing that, and I don't know if you could call it correct, but that's what works for me.

 Do you ever get bored playing rockabilly-type stuff? If not, how do you keep your playing fresh within that style? —*JUSTICE EDWARDS*

I always mix in new things, new influences. There are so many different styles you can play in that genre. I mean, I'm a rockabilly guitar player, but I'm influenced by all American musical styles, like jazz, blues, country and rock and roll. So the way to keep from getting bored from playing one particular genre of music is to mix in other styles.

BUDDY
GUY

What was it about those old blues players that gave their records such a warm, honest sound?

—TODD WALKER

Again, I go to the technology. What you hear on those old recordings is exactly what the artists were doing in the studio. Nothing was added to make my sound perfect; it was just a guitar, an amplifier and a microphone. Nowadays, you've got so many buttons to push in a recording studio, I wouldn't know what to do with it.

Q: **What was the hardest part for you on the road to becoming such an accomplished guitar player?** —*STEPHEN LANG*

The rhythm. When I first came to Chicago in 1957, they was making fun of me! The late Junior Wells used to say, "You can play, but you ain't got no time." And I was like, "What the hell is that?" So [*drummer*] Fred Below and me would go play, just drums and guitar, and he told me, "Every time you hear me make this turnaround, that's the end of a chorus." And that's when I started learning rhythm.

Q: **When I play the blues, I find myself repeating too much. How did you learn to keep your licks and phrases different and interesting?** —*TOMMY LEE ATKINS*

I think you just need to let someone listen to you. Something new is coming out each and every time you play, but you can't hear it. I know that I couldn't hear it in my own playing. I used to throw my guitar in a corner and attempt to walk away from it. I'd be thinking, You'll never get it! I felt like I was at a stand still, that I wasn't learning anymore. But every time someone else heard me, they could hear things in my playing that I couldn't. Man, all you've gotta do is keep playing that guitar.

Q: **Of all the musicians you've heard over the years, who stands out in your mind as being underrated and underappreciated?** —*PATRICK FISCHER*

Earl Hooker. I tried to figure out slide guitar after I'd heard Elmore James play slide, but people kept tellin' me to go hear Earl Hooker play. I said, "Who is that?" 'cause he didn't have no records out. But one night I walked into a club and I heard this melody, like someone was singing. I said, "Who is that singing?" and someone said, "No one. That's Hooker playing the slide." I had a slide in my pocket, and even before I got introduced to him, I just walked up and gave it to him.

Q: **Buddy, some of my favorite albums of yours are the ones you made for Vanguard Records, like *A Man and the Blues*. How do you feel about that period in your career?** —*RICK LONGLEY*

My feeling was that Muddy Waters had made Chess Records a success, so where could I fit in? When I went to Vanguard, I was able to have some impact finally, because I had a little more freedom there. When the British guys started hearing my Vanguard recordings, they started cranking up too. Even so, I still had one hand tied behind me.

DEAR GUITAR HERO

KIRK
HAMMETT

OF METALLICA

Vanguard wanted that Muddy Waters kind of "real" blues, and they wouldn't let me turn it up like I was doing when I played live.

 Q: **What was the Chicago club scene like in the late Fifties and early Sixties? And what did audiences expect from their entertainers?**

—JANIE REAGAN

The audiences in the clubs were 99.9 percent black, and when you played for black audiences, you had to put on a *show*, just like Little Richard or James Brown did. It was a *show* when guys like that played, and that's what people went to see. The performers danced, and they wanted you to be into it. It wasn't a Nat King Cole or Frank Sinatra type thing where you could stand there and stop people in their tracks and make 'em just listen to your voice. We had to make 'em look and say, 'What is he *doing*?' "

Q: *Master of Puppets* **is considered one of the greatest metal albums, a classic album in a classic style that inspired generations of musicians. Do you think that style of epic, blistering, solo-filled metal will ever become popular again?** —*MATT HEAFY (TRIVIUM)*

In retrospect, *Master of Puppets* is my favorite Metallica album, and I would like to see other people make more albums like it. While a lot of metal bands have taken the basic elements we established on *Master* and expanded on them, no one has yet to make an album as good. At least I haven't heard it yet. But then again, I'm biased. [*laughs*]

I'm not saying that *Master* was the peak of metal or anything; there have been a lot of great metal albums since we recorded it. All I'm saying is that, from song to song, *Master of Puppets* is very consistent. It stays within the niche it carved for itself. And that niche is either very big, because of its range of influence, or very narrow, because I haven't really heard any album like it since.

Q: **When** *Master of Puppets* **was finished, did the band realize it had created such an important piece of heavy metal history?**
—*MARK MORTON (LAMB OF GOD)*

Master of Puppets wasn't written with that intention; we just wanted to make the best album we could. For us, it was just another Metallica album. We had put out *Kill 'Em All*, and it was a great album. We put out *Ride the Lightning*, and it seemed to have all the elements of *Kill 'Em All* and then some. Then we put out *Master*, and we were very proud of it. It was like having another feather in our cap.

At that point, we were firing on all cylinders and the songs just kept coming, so we really seized the moment. After we finished the album, we went straight out on tour. We were very intent on getting the music out to the people and touring as much as humanly possible. But Cliff [*Burton*]'s death changed all of that.

None of us had any idea *Master of Puppets* would still sound fresh after 20 years. I mean, I put it on the other day and the album's sound, songs and concepts are just as relevant today as they were back then.

Q: **How did you feel about having the band's inner workings and conflicts exposed to the world in** *Some Kind of Monster***?** —*JULIO NAVARRE*

I'm a very private person who enjoys his solitude, so I have my issues with the movie in that regard. At the same time, I think its great, 'cause it sheds light on what we went

67

through. It also sheds light on the benefits of psychotherapy. If watching the movie can help people see the light they need to see, then I think that's a beautiful thing. I don't care if my solitude and privacy are sacrificed if ultimately it helps people.

I've discovered that people tend to see us as we were in the movie, but the film doesn't truly represent us. It was filmed several years ago, and we've moved on since then. We've grown as people and changed since then.

Q: **Do you ever listen back to solos and cringe? If you could change any of your solos which one would it be?** —*JOHN KEMPAINEN (THE BLACK DAHLIA MURDER)*

Yeah, there are a few solos I listen to and think, What the *hell* was I trying to do there? [*laughs*] There definitely have been situations in the studio when we were running out of time or energy but we had to finish. Sometimes the art suffers because of the deadline, which always sucks.

There were a couple of solos on *Kill 'Em All* that were rushed, and I wish I could redo the solo on "Frayed Ends of Sanity" from …*And Justice for All*. I recorded that solo at four in the morning. I was exhausted, but we needed to finish because the next day we were leaving for the Monsters of Rock tour with Van Halen. I really wish I had time to go back and redo that one. But the funny thing is, I've run into people who say it's their favorite solo on that album.

Q: **Have you ever considered recording a solo album?** —*HARRY MEYERS*

Yeah. Eventually I'll record one, but right now my loyalties remain with Metallica. I've been writing music for Metallica for over 20 years, but obviously there are certain things I've written that don't belong on Metallica albums. As a result I have a small surplus of music.

But you know, if I put out a solo album, don't expect it to be a super-duty heavy metal shred album; it's gonna be something that you've never heard before, or at least something you'd never expect from me. Recently, I played with a contemporary classical string quartet in San Francisco named Flux. It was a collaborative piece, with two violins, viola, cello, classical guitar and me on electric guitar. I gotta say, I don't think I've ever heard anything like the stuff we were doing. I thought, Well if I ever do a solo album, maybe I'll do it with some classical players. But really, I'm only using this as an example to show that, if I put out a solo album, it'll be something very eclectic. I'd like

69

What do you think your life would be like if you were never in Metallica?

—DAVID HENRY

I would probably be running a comic store that sells monster and horror stuff. That's what I knew before I became a musician. I was a comic book–horror movie geek. [*laughs*] That was the direction my life was heading before I bought a guitar.

to share that side of my playing with people someday, but now is not the right time. My loyalty is to maintain the Metallica legacy.

Q: **If you only had one choice, which solo would you want to be remembered for?** —*GERRY LOPATE*

I don't know if it's my defining moment, but one of my very favorite guitar solos is the solo in "Hero of the Day." It just so melodic, and I feel I nailed the emotion that the song was trying to put across. It's not a ripping solo, but it fits the song 100 percent.

As far as ripping solos are concerned, I really like the one in "Wherever I May Roam." I have to say, though, I have a lot of favorite solos. [*laughs*] I really like the ones in "Master of Puppets" and "The Thing That Should Not Be," even though I spent only, like, half an hour on the latter. I also like "Devil's Dance" on *Reload*. That solo is really the first time I ever abused a Whammy Pedal, and I got some good results from it.

Q: **It seems that you lost interest in shredding in favor of a more bluesy type of feel and tone on *Load* and *Reload*. Did any particular influences or insights set you on this different path?** —*ALEJANDRO BOLANOS*

Yeah: Stevie Ray Vaughan. I really got into Stevie in '92–'93 and learned a bunch of his solos. After that, I just immersed myself in the blues and started listening to tons of Buddy Guy, Robert Johnson, T-Bone Walker, B.B. King, Freddie King, Albert King, Hendrix, Clapton, Paul Butterfield and Roy Buchanan. It really leaked into my playing.

Q: **There have been many theories spread on the internet about why you tape your hands. So once and for all, why *do* you do it?** —*JERRY GLASS*

If you look at the side of your hand, right below your pinkie, you'll see there are some wrinkle lines. At least there are on my hand... [*laughs*] Because of my playing style, I'm constantly hitting the strings and palm muting and, generally, beating up my right hand. Over the course of a tour, those wrinkles start busting open and bleeding. I put tape over the wrinkles so that they don't break open and bleed all over my guitar, 'cause if a string gets in there once your hand is cut—wow!—that stings! Plus, it lets me play faster since it reduces drag between my hand and the strings.

Once, when we were on tour, I looked out into the audience and saw a kid with both his hands taped like mine. I was cracking up so much I had to give him a backstage pass.

DEAR GUITAR HERO

DAVE
GROHL

OF FOO FIGHTERS

Q: **What gives you the most pleasure when performing onstage: playing guitar or drums?** —*SEAN ALLAIR*

They're entirely different. Being able to run around with my guitar and be the ringleader of this big circus is one thing, but being the *force* behind everyone on the drum set is probably where I feel most comfortable. I've *never* been afraid to play the drums. I'm not the greatest drummer in the world, but I do what I do and I'm not intimidated by a drum kit. Whereas the guitar…I feel like it's still a Rubik's Cube to me; it's still something of a mystery. It humbles me every day. So I'd have to say for pure pleasure's sake, going out with the drum set makes me feel pretty strong, and going out with a guitar makes me feel like a little schoolboy. [*laughs*]

Q: **What's your favorite piece of gear?** —*MARK BAXTER*

My Gibson Trini Lopez. I've used that guitar for every Foo Fighters album. It's a red model; I think it's a '66. It sounds great clean or dirty, and it has a great percussive cut to it. It sounds great through a Boogie, Marshall, Hiwatt, AC30… You can do *anything* with that guitar.

Q: **It's awesome that you play both guitar and drums. I also play both instruments. How do you manage to keep your chops up with both? I keep falling behind on drums.** —*KIERAN COOPER*

It's good for me to put down the guitar every once in a while. Because I find that when I come back to it after a month or so, I start from a new creative place. But if I don't get on a drum set every day, it's inevitable that I'm gonna lose chops and get outta shape; to play drums the way that I do, I have to be in pretty good physical shape. I can still *think* as the drummer I was before, but it's difficult to get back there physically. But with the guitar, I like to take breaks. Having played guitar for, like, 28 years now, it's nice to come back to it with a fresh perspective.

Q: **When was the first time being a musician got you laid?** —*JOEY JENNINGS*

I suppose I was 18 years old and on the road with my band Scream. I got with some chick in Chicago… I don't really remember. I mean, that was 20 fucking years ago! [*laughs*] But it sure didn't happen until I left home, because in the small town where I grew up it didn't matter if I was a musician or not. I was "that skinny kid from Springfield, Virginia." So I had to get in the van and get outta there to make that happen.

Your output has been tremendous. How do you keep coming up with lyrics for songs? I'm also a songwriter, and I'm having trouble writing lyrics. —*BEN DOUGLAS*

Lyrics aren't easy. They have to be real and come from something that's true. I'm not much of a storyteller with my lyrics; they're usually autobiographical. I think it's hard to write lyrics if you're not inspired by something. The process is about the search for inspiration. You don't have to be Keats or Thoreau in order to write something beautiful; anybody can say something real. You just have to find the things that really mean something to you.

 On "Everlong," you whisper random words during the bridge. According to foofighters.com, the words come from three spoken-word tracks that you scrambled together: a love letter being read, a reading from a technical manual and someone telling a story about a studio technician's father. What made you pick these three things? —*KEITH CHAMBERLAIN*

Ah, that's a secret I'll never tell. It's been a secret for years. That's like my *Da Vinci Code*. [*laughs*] No one will ever know!

 There are rumors that you and Zakk Wylde got into a fight. Is that true? —*MATT*

[*laughs*] No. I have actually never met Zakk. We do have the same birthday, though. [*laughs*] I think he was upset with me because I was asked to write a song for an Ozzy record. He wanted to kill me, I suppose. But I'm sure the two of us could make amends over a bottle of Crown Royal. I know a lot of musicians, and I don't know too many that don't like each other. You could put any 10 musicians in one room with a bottle of whiskey, and at the end of the day you would have yourself a best-friend club.

 When you started the Foo Fighters, you switched from playing drums to playing guitar and being a frontman. Did playing behind Kurt Cobain all those years inspire you to do that? —*GREGORY MCKAYE*

Not necessarily. But playing in Nirvana did inspire me to make better music. I never imagined myself as a frontman. That didn't happen until much later. The whole Foo Fighters thing was an experiment that started with a demo tape and later turned into a band. Simply playing in Nirvana was inspirational. I found that music could cross a lot

You've played with some amazing musicians throughout your career. But if you could play with any guitarist, who would it be?

—DAVE

I'd have to say Jimmy Page, because to me he's the ultimate guitar player. He's my favorite guitar player of all time, and I think he's a genius.

of boundaries and touch a lot of people. And Nirvana was a band that seemed to touch a whole lot of people.

Q: **What is your most embarrassing on-the-road moment?** —*MIKE IVANY*
Probably shitting myself in the van when I was in Scream because I had the flu. [*laughs*] I didn't tell anybody and tried to keep it cool until we got to the next rest stop so I could get rid of my shorts. It happens. [*laughs*] Ask any touring musician how many times they've shit their pants. Most everyone's done it at least once. [*laughs*]

Q: **What gets you pumped before a show?**—*ROBBY*
I do jump around a lot, because I like to break a sweat before I hit the stage. I used to crank Sepultura, Slayer's *Reign in Blood* or AC/DC's *Let There Be Rock*. Then I went through this one fucking phase where I listened to soft rock before going onstage [*laughs*], but it didn't end up working too well. I'd walk out there really mellow after listening to the fucking Doobie Brothers or whatever. But I don't do that anymore. Now it's more about having a laugh and a drink as you walk to the stage, just being in a good mood.

Q: **You have the whitest teeth in rock roll. Is it a genetic gift or good dentistry?** —*MARK JONES*
[*laughs*] That's not true. You know, my dentist has told me that I have really good teeth. I've never had braces. But unfortunately my two front teeth have been ground down over the past 13 years from being up against a microphone. If you look at them from the side, it looks like they've been grated away, like when you grate the rind off a lemon. That's what's happening to my teeth.

DICKEY BETTS

Q: Your beautiful instrumentals like "Jessica" and "In Memory of Elizabeth Reed" say so much without uttering a word. Do you set out to write an instrumental, or is the decision made as the song develops?
—*JOSHUA SMITH*

I set out to write them. It is a totally different approach. I don't really have a specific technique, but I put in hours of deliberation as to what notes should follow each other, in order to get the best phrase that will communicate an emotion and thought without words. One exception is "Revival," which was supposed to be an instrumental. As I was writing the thing, I got going and started singing, just screwing around. I liked the words that came out of my mouth, so I stopped working on it as an instrumental.

Q: Your guitar tone is amazing. What is your stage setup?
—*JOHN HENDERSON*

Equipment has its purposes when it comes to satisfying a guitarist's tone requirements. But having said that, players like me and Carlos Santana, and past greats like Jerry Garcia and Duane Allman, can pick up any guitar or plug into any rig and sound like ourselves. Your technique, vibrato and choice of melody have a lot to do with your sound.

Having said that, I'll point out the obvious: no professional guitarist uses transistor amps; you've got to use tubes. I think the biggest thing that makes my sound is that I use Lansing speakers, which are really clear but will distort when pushed. Other than that, I use stock Marshall amps that are biased for a little more treble, because the standard setting is pretty bassy. And I don't use a lot of outboard stuff. I'll sometimes use a wah, but in general I don't like pedals, because I'm trying to utilize the sound of a real good piece of wood: my Gibson Les Paul.

Q: I love the way you set up push-pull rhythms, as on "No One to Run With." Can you please describe that a bit? —*BOOGER NELSON*

Duane and I were very conscious of how a drummer plays rhythm on a snare drum by utilizing a lot of counterpoint and interplay. We would try to do the same thing with our dual rhythm parts. For instance, I could set something with a push on the 2 and 4 beats, and he would play on the 1 and 3. We were very aware of really letting each person's downbeat appear in different spots so they didn't get tangled up. That's because [*bassist*] Berry [*Oakley's*] playing was really busy, as well; he wasn't just playing the bass line. By working the rhythms like that, you create a back-and-forth feel, almost like a guy playing a snare drum with both hands.

Duane was really more adept at that type of thing than I was, because he had put in time doing session work. I learned a lot of that from him. "No One to Run With" is a newer song that utilizes some of the same ideas.

Q: **Can you recall anything that Duane Allman said about your playing?**
—DAVE LUCAS

We talked about guitars and playing constantly, so it's hard to recall any one thing, but Duane was always very complimentary to me. He would really get upset when people didn't recognize I was a lead guitar player. A lot of people assumed Duane was the lead player and I was the rhythm guy because of the name of the band and because he was so charismatic and I was more laid back. That really upset Duane. He would always say, "You don't realize this cat played that, not me. There's two guitar players in this damn band!" He would really stick up for me, going out of his way to make people aware we were twin guitars.

Q: **How did you and Duane work out your guitar harmonies?** *—TODD*

It was really natural. Duane would almost always wait for me or sometimes [*bassist Berry*] Oakley to come up with a melody, and then he would join in with the harmony. We did a lot of it on the fly. If I played a riff twice, the third time he would be right on it with the harmony. We almost never sat down and figured out the notes; we just did it. And if you listen carefully to a lot of the harmonies Duane played, it's not the correct notes you would choose if you wrote it out, but it always sounded great.

Q: **What was the biggest stylistic difference between how you and Duane played?** *—DARDEN COPELAND*

The perfect guitar voices we heard in our heads were polar opposites. He liked a real spitfire trebly sound, with staccato phrasing, and my thing was more of a rounded sound. That reflected itself in different ways and helped us develop a great sound together.

I play mostly on my neck pickup, and Duane always played his leads on the treble pickup. His melodic sense came mostly from jazz and urban blues, while mine came from country blues, with a strong element of string [*bluegrass*] music, because my dad played fiddle. Therefore, my phrasing had more of a looping style, while Duane's was more cutting. We were almost totally opposite, except we both knew the importance of phrasing. We didn't just ramble about.

What made you guys laugh when Jim Marshall shot the photo for the *At Fillmore East* album cover?

—KOSTAS XANTHAKIS

Jim wanted the light to be perfect, so we had to get up at daylight. We were all in a real grumpy mood, figuring it didn't make a damn bit of difference what time we took the picture. A dude Duane knew came walking down the sidewalk on his way home after working all night. Duane jumped up, ran over and got a joint from this guy, then ran back to take his place with the rest of us. He had just copped a toke and had a mischievous grin on his face. We all just cracked up. If you look, you can see Duane is hiding something in his hand.

What inspired you to write "Blue Sky," and did you play all the guitar parts on the recording? —*A.S.*

Hell no, I did not play all the guitar parts. Duane is very much on it. It was one of the last things he ever recorded. I wrote it for my wife at the time, who was Native American and whose name translated to "Blue Sky." It was originally a love song to her, but once I wrote it I realized how nice it would be to keep the vernacular "he's" and "she's" out and make it like you're thanking the spirit for the day.

 On the Allman Brothers' earliest recordings, you all sound like seasoned veterans. How were you able to become so proficient at such young ages? —*SCOTT TREZAK*

Man, I don't know. The young guys in my band ask me that all the time. For being such young cats, we really had some good players, and Duane and Berry Oakley had incredible leadership qualities. I was a couple of years older than everyone, but we were all basically kids. The only explanation I can give is that we were a nightclub band, not a garage band. We had brought ourselves up by actually playing in the bars in front of audiences, and that really gives you a lot more depth than if you just play in a studio or a garage before you make records.

Duane and Gregg were on the circuit as teenagers, and my first road gig came when I was 16, playing in a band that traveled to state fairs and such. We had a tent show called "Teen Beat," and we played on the midway. We did 15 30-minute shows a day, sometimes. We played stuff like Little Richard and Chuck Berry, and I did splits and duck walks. We would get on each other's shoulders, and we'd slide across the stage on our knees, wearing kneepads hidden under our pants. [*laughs*] All those gigs paid off.

DEAR GUITAR HERO

DUFF
McKAGAN

I saw Loaded live recently. What's that funny-looking Les Paul you're playing? —*JACK TEEGARDEN*

It's called a Burny. When Loaded went to Japan in 2000 or 2001, a Fernandes rep came to one of our gigs and brought one down. You can only get them in Japan, because of U.S. trademark laws. They're so close to a Les Paul they can't sell them here. I played it on a song or two that night in Japan, and it was the best-sounding fuckin' Les Paul I've ever played. And [*the Sex Pistols'*] Steve Jones was over there, the same trip. He's played nothing but that since, and he's a classic Les Paul guy. I now have four of those Burny guitars.

What are your musical guilty pleasures? —*JOHANNA BOEFE*

I've always been into, like, Prince and Cameo. I've always been that guy who will blast that stuff in the backstage room, and everyone else is going, "*Fuuuck*, dude, come on!" I also like OutKast, and I like Katy Perry, because of my daughters. My 11-year-old turned me on to Shiny Toy Guns. I think they're great.

Why did you originally pick up bass? —*ED DONNELLY*

I played drums, but my drum kit was a piece of shit. Since I was moving by myself to L.A. I couldn't take too much stuff, so I sold my drum kit for probably 70 bucks. I also sold my guitar amp.

There weren't a lot of good bass players in L.A., so I thought, I'll do that—I'll get my foot in the door and then figure out what I'm gonna do. And one of the first ads I answered was from Slash, who was looking for a bass player. We met at a restaurant, and the rest, as they say, is history.

What did you think of *Chinese Democracy*? —*PAT*

Why do people ask me that question? My opinion means nothing. Like anybody else, I listened to it. I love Axl's voice, and there are songs I like and songs I don't like. But that could be any record.

I read that the Guns track "It's So Easy" was autobiographical about your life. Was there anything you left out? —*SLPN0T22*

I probably left out a lot of the gory details, but I think the important stuff is all in there: the debauchery of sex and drugs and rock and roll. That song sums it up much more than I'd intended. The day I wrote it, my friend West Arkeen [*co-writer of several Guns N'*

Who was an easier frontman to work with: Axl Rose or Scott Weiland?
—LISA D.

They're both [*pauses*] complicated guys to work with, for sure. At any given time, Axl's really easy to work with. At other times, he's really difficult, and the same can be said for Scott. Scott is definitely more self-destructive, and therefore probably a little harder.

Roses songs] had taught me open E tuning. And right there at that moment, that song came out—the melody and the lyrics.

 I read that GN'R recorded a track you wrote called "Cornshucker" for the *GN'R Lies* album, but you didn't put it out because it was too dirty. What do you remember about that song? —*JAMIE PENDERTON*

I had just listened to a Mentors record. They played what you might call "abusive sex rock." They were really sick dudes. GN'R were recording at Sound City and laying down every song we knew in a 48-hour period. We recorded something like 30 songs. At one point, I was out in the main tracking room playing a guitar and singing a song that I was making up on the spot, and Axl goes, "Dude, what the hell is that?" And I said, "It's called 'Cornshucker'! I just wrote it." He loved it. We were just fucking around and laughing. The song was too brutal to put out, even for us.

 Is it true you were one of the last people to see Kurt Cobain alive? What happened? —*MIKE BELSEN*

A lot's been made out of that. Sometimes I wish that was never found out. We were on the same plane together coming back from L.A. to Seattle. I was in no frame of mind to be insightful; I was fucked up out of my mind. This was near the end of *my* run, too. I think it was about two months or a month before my pancreas gave up. Kurt had just left Exodus [*Recovery Center*], and we were both drinking. We were two travelers in the same situation, completely constrained by our addictions. So we had a lot in common because of that.

And that's what we were talking about on the trip back. He had just bought a house, and he was going home alone. And I had a house, and my buddy came to pick me up from the airport. At the last minute, I thought about inviting him over to the house, but he was gone. His bag came before mine, and he said, "See ya." And that was it. It's not really that great of a story. And I feel guilty even talking about it.

87

DEAR GUITAR HERO

ERIC JOHNSON

Q: **What is the greatest misconception about you and your music?**
—RAY WILSON

That's hard to say. The music business constructs an image of an artist based on what it wants, and that image tends to stick around. Sometimes, no one bothers to look between the cracks to see if the image resembles the truth. That can be frustrating, but it's also the responsibility of the artist to obliterate that image by making something powerful enough to dispel it. There is certainly a stigma to being a "guitar hero." But I know what music turns me on and how I want to fit into the world of guitar players, and I try to keep on that journey with everything I do, without worrying too much about how others perceive me.

Q: **What would you suggest for someone on a limited budget who wants that trademark Texas-sized Eric Johnson tone?** *—VOLTAGE*

Good tone, whether it's based around mine or not, begins with a versatile amplifier. I recommend a silverface Fender Twin or Pro Reverb, especially if you can get one with a nice old Jensen speaker. You want an amp with pure tone, something with which you can create a clean and simple sound. From there, you can add an overdrive pedal or any other effect you want, but you have to begin with a good clean sound. To make another point, I think people overemphasize the importance of gear in their search for tone. Your sound comes from how you pick and dampen the strings, and from your attack, as much as anything.

Q: **Will we be seeing a concert DVD from you any time soon?**
—CHARLES JOHNSON

I hope so, though I don't have any plans for one at this time. I just finished an instructional DVD on which I explain the 10 essential points to creating great music. I tried to keep it simple and straightforward, without getting into too much flamboyant technique or gear.

Q: **Who are some of your favorite classical composers?** *—JOE SWEEP*

Aaron Copland, Maurice Ravel, Béla Bartók, Claude Debussy, Igor Stravinsky and Mozart. Franz Liszt and Chopin are way up there. Georg Telemann is a very interesting guy, and I also love George Gershwin.

You're famous for obsessing about your tone, but have you learned to relax and let the music and ideas flow and let go of the technical stuff?

—MIKE KRETZ

I've gotten better. There is certain music I would like to advance and implement on guitar, and pulling it off is a real challenge, so it's hard not to obsess over it. If you want to make the guitar into a sustaining, ferocious sound, you have to use distortion, which is a beautiful thing, but it creates all sort of problems. Having said all that, I'm not obsessing as much as I used to.

Q: **Was Chet Atkins an influence on your hybrid-picking technique?**
—*SANDY HALLIDAY*

He was, but Chet is so special to me that I've always tried to just enjoy his music and not dissect it. I like the overall effect of his playing, in a reverent way, and I don't want to turn hearing his music into a workshop. However, a lot of Chet's picking technique came from Merle Travis, who I have studied pretty intensely, so I'm sure I have a lot of Chet in my technique, whether I realize it or not.

Q: **I've heard about your "koto" technique. What is it?** —*STRATOBLASTER*

It's really pretty simple. You just fret the note with the index finger of your right hand, then pick right behind it with your right hand. Because you're picking so close to the fret, the picked string sounds thin and twangy, like a koto [*a traditional Japanese stringed instrument*]. I'll also place my left hand on the string to stretch it. This also allows me to pull off my right-hand finger; since my left-hand finger is still in place, doing this can create a nice pull-off sound.

Q: **Why are there no string trees on the new signature Strat?** —*BEN FORD*

String trees hinder a guitar's ability to stay in tune, but they're necessary because of the headstock's pitch—that is, the degree to which the headstock is tilted. We slightly changed the pitch, which, in combination with the staggered tuning keys, allowed us to eliminate the trees. As a result, you can actually use the guitar's vintage tremolo system a small amount without the guitar going out of tune.

Q: **Rosewood or maple fretboards, and why?** —*FRANK STOKES*

Maple seems to have a purer fundamental tone, and that's what I generally use, though I think rosewood has a better rhythm tone for complex harmonics. I own one rosewood Strat, and I like it.

Q: **What is in your rig?** —*NIKILI KITE*

It's very simple. I have three amp setups that produce tones ranging from really clean to very saturated, though I never use them all at once. The first setup consists of two Fender Twins with a Princeton Chorus stereo chorus. The second is a Marshall 100-watt set around 7.5 to 8 on the first channel for a Keith Richards–style crunch rhythm. I also have a Fuzz Face on there, so I can also kick into a Hendrix-style sound. The third

You have a very unique style. Who were your primary influences?

—PAUL CHASE

When I was a kid, my dad played all types of music. It ingrained in me the idea that all music has something to offer. If you listen to the spirit behind the music, you can connect the dots between players like John McLaughlin, Jimi Hendrix, Jeff Beck, Eric Clapton, Charlie Christian and Wes Montgomery…not to mention Mozart, Debussy and Gershwin. They were all big influences to me.

setup is a Marshall with a Tube Driver, for extra saturation; the Marshall's volume is all the way up, and the EQ is set for a classic Clapton tone. Occasionally, I use a CryBaby wah with any of these, but I run it through a rack.

Q: Given your penchant for vintage Strats, how do you manage extraneous noise at high-gain levels? —ANONYMOUS

The noise is pretty bad. I don't like it, but you have to pick your poison. I've chosen to wrestle the beast, but I would really like to slay it. I'm working with Fender's Michael Braun to create a hum-canceling pickup that sounds like a single-coil. I think he may well crack that nut. In the meantime, the middle pickup on my signature Strat is wrapped differently from the other two, and I can always use it if the noise is overwhelming.

Q: I was amazed by the cascading harmonics you demonstrated on your instructional video. What is the origin of this delicate technique and how long did it take to master it? —CHARLES MANTHY

I don't know the origin, but [*seven-string jazz fingerstyle guitarist*] Lenny Breau made it popular, and that's where I got it, though someone may well have done it before him. As for mastering it, it's an ongoing process, especially if you change the harmonics' voicing. Just break it down and take it step by step.

Q: How did you get that fantastic liquid tone on "Cliffs of Dover," and was that one cohesive solo or an amalgam? —J. PARADIS

I played a Gibson ES-335 through a 100-watt Marshall. I put it all together by playing sections, then dropping them in and connecting them into a seamless whole.

Q: During the Seventies, you and Stevie Ray Vaughan were Austin's primary guitar-slingers. Was there a lot of competition between you? —STEPHEN HUNG

No. We were playing different kinds of music. I always enjoyed hearing Stevie and his group play. It was nice to have him around in the clubs. You could go see him every night, and his greatness was readily apparent.

DEAR GUITAR HERO

ALEXI LAIHO

OF CHILDREN OF BODOM

Some of your solos are insane, like the one in "Mask of Sanity." Do you ever have trouble pulling off certain songs live? —*TODD SKOLDENT*

No, it's not usually a problem for me, and I've never had to rearrange a part to make it work. But some of our songs—especially the ones on *Are You Dead Yet?*—have a lot of crazy guitar rhythms with different vocal rhythms over them. I rehearse those parts by playing the riff slowly and saying the lyrics on top of it until I can play it correctly and at the proper speed.

 Do you think studying classical guitar can help you become a sick shredder? —*SWANO*

I've never studied classical guitar, but before I started playing guitar, I played the violin and took classical violin lessons. I'm sure classical guitar lessons would help with a player's fretting hand, but learning to pick would be a whole different deal.

 When you were younger, how often would you practice and how would you structure your practice sessions? Do you still practice now? —*TROY*

When I was younger and learning how to play, I spent a crazy amount of time practicing—six and sometimes eight hours a day. It varies these days. If I haven't played in a couple days, I have to warm up for about an hour. And even though I play all the time, I still try to learn new shit.

 Who are some of your musical influences? Anybody we might not expect? —*TIMOTHY FISCHER*

All the Ozzy guitar players—Randy Rhoads, Jake E. Lee, Zakk Wylde—as well as Paul Gilbert and Steve Vai. And here's somebody you might not expect: Mark Knopfler. My dad was always blasting Dire Straits, so it was the first real guitar music that I got into. Knopfler has his own style, and I love his playing. He's brilliant.

 I suffer from bouts of RSI (repetitive strain injury) and tendonitis brought on by hours of practicing. Have you had any playing injuries? I think I've seen you wearing a pink cast. —*VERE H-T*

Yeah, I had a cast on my right arm for seven weeks, but it wasn't caused by practicing. I was drunk as hell, and—don't even ask me why—I was standing on top of a car. It was wintertime and the roof of the car was really slippery, so of course I fell off. When I woke up, I had a super-gnarly black eye and three broken bones in my arm, plus I needed stitches.

95

As for guitar-related injuries, I did get tendonitis once, five years ago. I had to stop playing for a few weeks. When I started again, I had to relearn how to pick because my old technique was causing the injury. Since I've changed picking techniques, everything's been fine.

Q: **Why did you make those lame comments about Dream Theater in *Guitar World* [April 2005]? You're a fine player, but comments like those just make people lose respect for you. Did you know it caused a big stir? —*BRAD BAILEY***

[*Laiho indirectly called Dream Theater guitarist John Petrucci "super lame" and said of the group's songs, "It's not even music; it's sports."*]

Fuck. [*laughs*] Well, apparently it did. First of all, I think it's really funny that people trash bands and musicians every day on the internet, and nobody gives a shit. But once you say something like that—which wasn't even too bad—in a magazine, all of a sudden you're the biggest dick on earth.

But truthfully, I don't know why I said that. I was having a bad day or something. Obviously, John Petrucci is a better guitar player than I am, and it's not my place to talk shit about him.

Q: **What's up with that "Smoke Crack and Worship Satan" shirt in the *Hate Crew Death Roll* booklet? Are you poking fun, or do you hit the pipe and love the devil? —*JOSHUA STEWART***

[*laughs*] It's a funny shirt! Whenever I see a very offensive shirt, I'm compelled to buy it. Actually, my ex-girlfriend got that one for me. But for the record, I do not smoke crack or worship Satan.

Q: **What was your most embarrassing moment onstage? —*ALLAN***

We were playing a festival in Spain or someplace and were about to play the song "Hate Crew Deathroll." I was trying to pump up the crowd by being all badass and saying, "I wanna see a fucking pit with this next song!" But as I was trying to introduce the song, something happened and I couldn't get the words out of my mouth. It came out as, "The next song is 'Crew...Death...Hate...Roll.'" I was stuttering like a fucking retard. I felt like such an asshole.

GARY
ROSSINGTON

OF LYNYRD SKYNYRD

Q: When you formed the Rossington-Collins Band after the Skynyrd plane crash, did you really talk to [*Bad Company's*] Paul Rodgers about being the singer? —*ANONYMOUS*

Yes, and he was interested, though he was busy with Bad Company and a solo album. Also, we really felt that if we had a male singer, the comparisons to Lynyrd Skynyrd would be constant and unfair—and that would have happened even if we had Paul McCartney singing. Ronnie really admired Paul Rodgers, and he styled a lot of his singing after him, but it made more sense for us to go with a woman to make it clear this was a different band.

Q: You guys are reputed to have been serious brawlers back in the day. How about one good story. —*ROBERT CARVER*

Oh, man, there are so many. One time, we were playing four or five sets at a Jacksonville bar called the Beachcomber Lounge, and every break we'd go out back and smoke a cigarette or something else and cool off for 15 minutes. One time, five or six sailors came back there and started messing with us. We were sort of freaked out, so we started walking away, but they came at us. We were right by our van, so Ronnie grabbed a tire iron that expanded outward when snapped. He whipped it out to five or six feet and started swinging it around and bashing them pretty good. Suddenly, we were chasing sailors all over Forsythe Street. Then we went right back in and started playing, bloody knuckles and all.

Q: Gary, is the SG you play during "Free Bird" the same one you've been playing since back in the day? Also, do you play your original Les Paul? —*SAM BRUGGEMAN*

No. I have the originals but I retired them because I didn't want them to get hurt, broken or stolen—which happened to the SG once, though luckily I got it back. I use my Gibson signature models now and they are great.

Q: What is that white thing you put under the nut when playing slide? Also, what kind of pick, slide and strings do you use? —*ALAN PRICE*

That's just a little piece of guitar cord. I use it only on "Free Bird." It goes back to when I started playing slide: I'd fret out from pressing too hard on the bottle. So I jammed a screwdriver under the nut, to raise the strings, and after a while I switched to using that

PHOTO BY TRAVIS SHINN

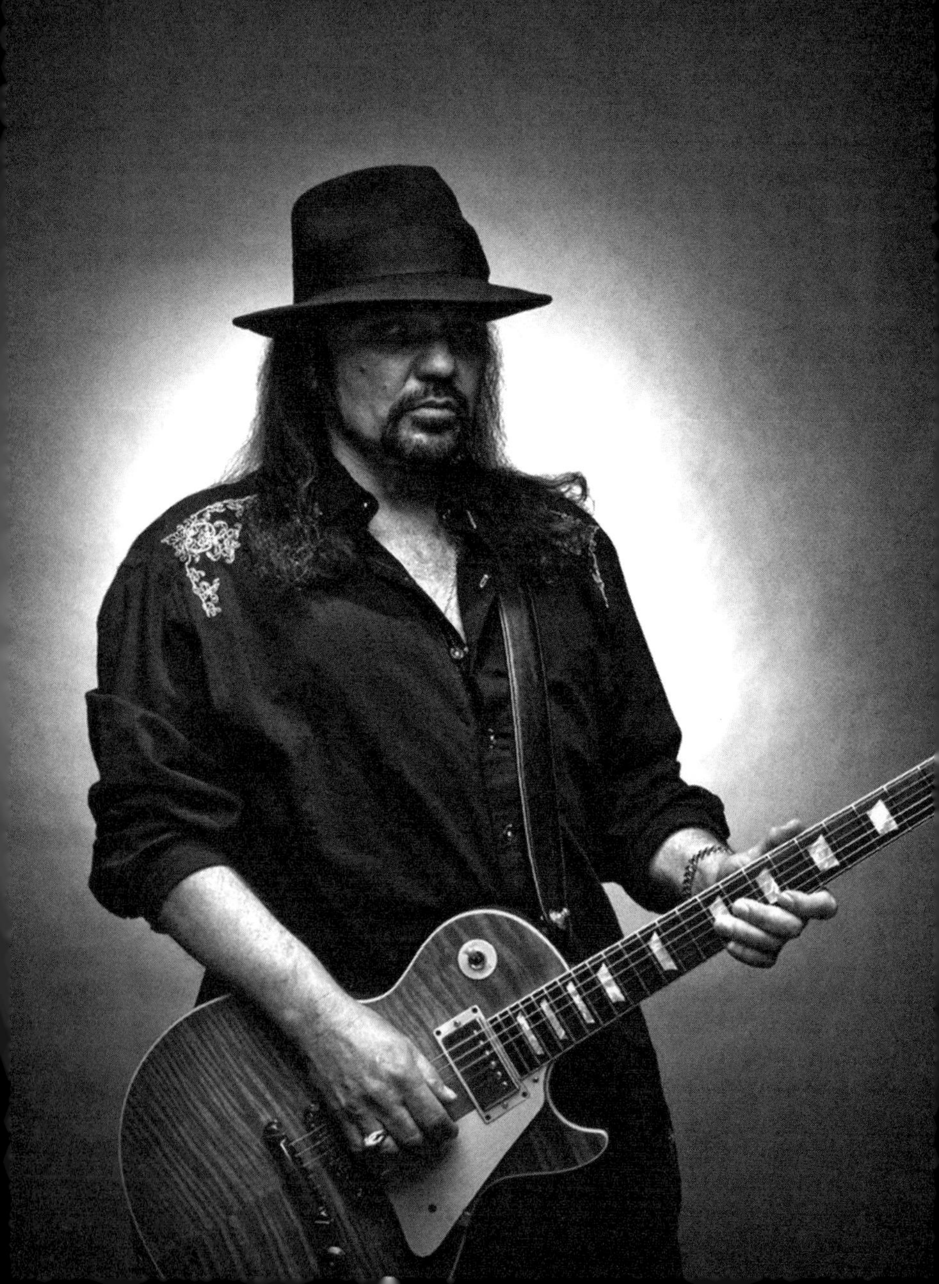

bit of cord. Eventually, I was able to play without fretting out, but I still use the cord, just out of habit. But only on that song.

I use Dean Markley and Gibson strings and a tiny, little green pick as well as our custom picks, which are Fender mediums. For slide, I use a Coricidin bottle, like Duane Allman did.

Q: **Who played the awesome solo on "Sweet Home Alabama"?**
—*ALEX THOMPSON*

Ed King played that on a Strat. The solo is in G, even though the song is in D—it's just D, C, G. That drove [*producer*] Al Kooper nuts. He kept saying it was in the wrong key. He eventually went into the studio and cut his own solo in D, and a nice little argument ensued. Obviously, he lost—and obviously we were right! Ed nailed it.

Q: **Was you smashing your new car into an oak tree while driving drunk really the inspiration for "That Smell"? What other songs were inspired by personal experiences?** —*RICH MURPHY*

Yeah, "That Smell" was a true story, unfortunately. A lot of the songs were true like that. Ronnie took most of his lyrics from life experiences. "Gimme Three Steps" was about an incident when Ronnie went into a bar to talk to this girl. Allen and I were underage so we waited in the car and Ronnie came running out with this redneck chasing him waving a gun because he didn't like him talking to his girl. He jumped in and we took off, then Ronnie wrote the song. "Double Trouble" was all stuff that occurred, because Ronnie got thrown in jail more than once for refusing to leave bars, being drunk and disorderly and stuff like that.

Q: **Do you use pedals to get your classic distortion or is it straight through the amp?** —*WAYNE MACK*

It's all from the amp. I have this 1971 Peavey Mace and I just love the dirty sound it has always given me. We just change the tubes and keep the wires going and it keeps sounding great.

Q: **Who played the solos and fills on *Street Survivor*'s "One More Time"?**
—*DAN KUSHNER*

I played the solos and Ed played slide. That song was not cut during the *Street Survivors* sessions—it was from '71. We put it on there because we liked it and had never used it for some reason.

 Q: **Who are your primary influences?** —*AARON SKIDMORE*
Duane Allman and all the English cats: Jeff Beck, Keith Richards, the Beatles, Eric Clapton and Jimmy Page.

Q: **How do you manage to play such high-energy licks and remain so stoic and stone-faced? Are you detached from what's coming through the amp?** —*ANONYMOUS*
I don't know. It's just what I do—stand there and wail. I'm almost in a daze. A lot of people jump around and make faces, but it's distracting to me. I guess I'm just from the old school.

Q: **What were some of the difficulties involved with having three lead guitar players?** —*TODD MOHR, BIG HEAD TODD AND THE MONSTERS*
Other than fighting to death over who got to solo? We started the band when we were 14 or 15 and Allen Collins and I really did fight over solos, but it boiled down to whoever could play a part best, played it. Ed King played bass on the first record so we didn't have three lead players until Leon Wilkeson, who had quit, came back to play bass and we moved Ed over to guitar. Then it was a like a battle of guitars, but we all respected each other and knew who could play a certain part best.

Q: **Was the "Free Bird" guitar solo a single amazing take or did you have a game plan before recording it?** —*JON GUTWILLIG, THE DISCO BISCUITS*
It was a solid game plan. That was Allen Collins' solo all the way. We "rehearsed" the song by playing it in clubs and dances for a year or two so he had the solo down cold. He knew what he was doing every note of the way.

 Q: **How did you guys come up with parts and make them work with three guitars? Did it just happen by feel and evolve over time or did you sit down and write things out?** —*CHUCK GARVEY, MOE.*
It was done by feel when we wrote the songs but then we all had our parts and we played them live so everything meshed and we didn't get in each others' way. We worked them

out and rehearsed them a lot. Take "Sweet Home Alabama"—it is actually three parts that fit together like a puzzle and none of them would sound right played alone. Playing with three leads requires more thought and you can't all play full chords or try to solo all the time.

Q: **When you were recording "Free Bird" was anyone foolish enough to say, "Hey you can't do that—that's *too* much guitar." Also, do you remember how you got the guitar sound on tape?** —*CHARLIE HITCHCOCK, PARTICLE*

Yeah, they did actually say that. Everybody, including the record company, our producer and our manager, said it was too long, no one will ever play it, you have to cut it. But we wouldn't do it. We rebelled and said, "Fuck it. We don't care if anyone plays it—this is the song." They put out single versions with 10- and 20-second solos, which we had nothing to do with.

As for how we recorded it, Allen and I both doubled our parts, then Allen did a third take. We did all that by feel, without even listening because we knew the song so well by then. When his second solo comes in it is a little offbeat so it sounds like two guitarists, but it's all Allen.

DEAR GUITAR HERO

CHAD
KROEGER

OF NICKELBACK

You've been moving toward a harder sound ever since *Silver Side Up*. What prompted you to change your style? —*JEREMY*

We have moved in a heavier direction, but we've also moved into more melodic territory, too. Nickelback's fan base is just so broad, it's impossible to keep everyone happy with one style of music. And we like keeping the fans happy, so we try to go all over the map, mixing the straight-up rockers with the really heavy shit and the melodic stuff, too.

 I was really touched by your Dimebag Darrell tribute, "Side of a Bullet," from *All the Right Reasons*. How did he influence you? —*MATT EVERSON*

Darrell was a very technical player, and I appreciate that. And due to the fact that he and his brother, Vinnie [*Paul, Pantera and Damageplan drummer*], had played together for so long, their timing and precision were absolutely amazing. There was no sloppiness; it was all surgical precision.

 Did you ever get your ass burned by the massive pyro on your *Silver Side Up* tour? Those flames shooting up through the stage were awesome. —*BUSTER DAILY*

[*laughs*] There were a couple of times when I thought the flames were going to melt right through my shirt. We couldn't wear certain types of clothing onstage because they would disintegrate if we got too close to the flames. But we've never had an incident with our pyro. Our track record is clean.

 I love your tone. Could you please describe your current live setup, including pickup and strings? —*DON BUTTACCIO*

I use Paul Reed Smiths, some with EMGs and some with stock Paul Reed Smith pickups. I run them through Triple Rectifiers going through Mesa and Marshall cabs simultaneously. That way, you get Mesa's huge low end and Marshall's great midrange bite. I play with Ernie Ball strings, and I use different gauges depending on the guitar. Some go as large as .070s.

 I'm in a band that's been waiting a long time to get signed. Got any advice for a fellow Canadian? —*DEREK BRYSON*

If at first you don't succeed, try, try again. You may be sitting on some songs that you think are the best, but if everybody's heard them and nobody's chomping at the bit to

I love your heavy riffs. What artists influenced you in that particular area?
—TOM WINRICK

When I'm writing a heavy riff, two people always come to mind: Dimebag Darrell and James Hetfield.

pick them up, don't hold onto them; go back to the drawing board and write some new tunes. Of course, that's my advice if your goal is a record deal. If you love those songs, then you have to go the independent route: self-finance the whole record and then hit the road and tour your independent album.

Q: **You have a knack for knowing when to play a solo and when not to. How do you decide what songs and passages deserve those extra flourishes and which don't?** —*GENE*

I just feel it. When it feels like you need a guitar solo, then you gotta play one. Or you gotta call up a buddy like Billy Gibbons and have him play a solo for you! [*laughs*]

Q: **The song "Throw Yourself Away," from *The Long Road*, is a powerful statement against killing babies. Are you pro-choice or pro-life?** — *KRYSTOF LEFTLIEN*

First, let's clarify something: that song's not about killing babies; it's about a specific incident when a girl gave birth in the bathroom during her prom, dumped the baby in a garbage can and then went back to dancing like nothing happened. This is not a debate about at what point a cell has a soul. That baby was alive; she could've given it up for adoption. But due to the overwhelming embarrassment she felt, she chose homicide. I'm against incidents like that.

But am I pro-choice or pro-life? I'm probably gonna piss off a lot of people, but I think it's a woman's choice and she should be able to do what she wants to with her body.

Q: **What do you turn to when you're in need of inspiration?** —*JAMES T.*

My bong. [*laughs*] It gets harder and harder to find topics to write about. You can always write about love, 'cause everyone can relate—it's one of the most powerful feelings in the world. But you've just gotta be creative about it.

107

GLENN TIPTON

&

K.K. DOWNING

OF JUDAS PRIEST

Q: If you were stranded on an island for the rest of your life, what one guitar, amp and effect would you want to bring? —*STU*

DOWNING Well, I'd definitely take my '67 Flying V and any amp by Marshall. And I think I'd go for the Hendrix effect setup: a Cry Baby and a Fuzz Face. Then I'd spend the rest of my time on the island trying to get Hendrix's sound and play like him! [*laughs*]

Q: Glenn, I read that you used to gut your onstage guitars so that your pickups were wired directly to the output and the knobs were just for show. Is this true? If so, why did you do that? —*T. MARK BARTLEY*

TIPTON I've never used the tone controls on any guitar. I can get all the tone from the neck or bridge pickups. I've always found that the more wiring you've got in the guitar, the worse off it is. For that reason, I rip most of the controls out of the guitar so the pickups are wired to the output jack. The sound might not be absolutely spot-on when compared to what you'd require in the studio, but a touring guitar is different from a studio guitar: it has to be an easily replaceable working tool, and it needs to be robust enough to get me through the tour. I never want to take anything onstage that I'm scared to lose or break. I just need a workhorse guitar, and for me the best-sounding workhorses are the ones without the frills.

Q: During the years vocalist Rob Halford was out of the band, did you ever think you would play music with him again? —*JOHN LEHRER*

DOWNING For the first couple of years I thought, He'll be back soon. It's only a matter of time. But after eight or 10 years I started thinking, Maybe this isn't gonna happen.

TIPTON I don't believe I ever stopped to analyze whether or not Rob would come back, but I think deep down inside I always knew we would get back together.

Q: What guitarists influenced you the most before Judas Priest got started? —*FRANK PROFACI*

DOWNING Hendrix had the biggest influence on me. I was fortunate to see him a bunch of times, and he was an absolute god—even going back to the very first time he appeared in England, when everybody else thought he was so uncouth and unacceptable. After Hendrix there was Ritchie Blackmore, Rory Gallagher, Jeff Beck, Jimmy Page, Alvin Lee... The list of great players from that era just goes on and on.

TIPTON My main influence was Hendrix, too, but more than anybody, Rory Gallagher

109

From left: Downing, Rob Halford and Tipton

was the guy responsible for me picking up the guitar. Before I was interested in music as a career or could even play the guitar, I used to go and watch him at a Birmingham [*England*] club called Mothers. To see Gallagher play his battered old Stratocaster through a Rangemaster [*treble booster*] and an AC30... His energy just blew my mind.

 How did you break the news to [*Tim*] "Ripper" Owens that [*original singer*] Rob Halford was returning to the band in 2003 after more than 10 years? And how did he take it? —*IAN SHERRY*

TIPTON There was a lot of demand for Rob to come back; a lot of people were pushing for it. So we chewed it over and decided that the best thing for the band would be to

110

reunite with him. We first broke the news to Ripper through a joint email, and then we all individually telephoned him. To his credit, Tim came back and said he agreed with it. He's always been a big fan of Priest and was a real gentleman about it. He stepped aside in the best possible way.

For five years, he had a great platform from which to show his own talents, and he did so extremely well. Nobody in this world could've done what Tim did. Nobody. And it's put him in good stead for his own career. I'm sure Tim will have success in his own right. He certainly deserves it.

 It sounds like you double the guitars at the beginning of "Electric Eye." Do you both play different pinch harmonics? That part is amazing and I'm having trouble nailing it. —*ZACK LARSON*

DOWNING Yeah, we both play different parts. But it's been such a long time since we did the original recording. Now it's just one of those things we do...it's so familiar I don't even think about it. I could probably do it in my sleep! [*laughs*]

 The Allman Brothers Band are usually credited with inventing twin lead guitars in rock. You did the same in metal. Did you ever listen to bands like the Allmans and Lynyrd Skynyrd back then? —*TOM MARKON*

DOWNING Yeah, of course I listened to them. When I was growing up, I was aware of the American movement—the James Gang, the Allman Brothers, the Doobie Brothers, the Grateful Dead and Alice Cooper. But I preferred the English style—Deep Purple, Sabbath and the like. It felt more raw, bluesy and progressive. Those West Coast bands seemed too melodic for me, I guess.

 Judas Priest were a key band in the New Wave of British Heavy Metal. At the time, did you feel you were part of a movement? Was there camaraderie or competition between you guys and, say, Dave Murray and Adrian Smith from Iron Maiden? —*JERRY EGGERS*

DOWNING I tend to perceive metal's evolutionary scale somewhat differently. The first wave consisted of bands like Black Sabbath and Deep Purple. Then there was the second wave of Judas Priest, Scorpions, UFO, et cetera, followed by the third wave of bands: Iron Maiden, Def Leppard, Saxon, and so on. Iron Maiden did their first U.K. and American tours supporting Priest—we were established headliners, and they were

I don't often hear you guys mentioned along with other guitar greats, like Van Halen, Kirk Hammett, Zakk Wylde and Steve Vai, though you guys set the bar high by pioneering an entire style and genre. Does that bother you? Do you think it's because there were always two of you, rather than just one guy to hold up and glorify?

—BRIAN

DOWNING I would say that's a fair comment. Both Glenn and I share a role, whereas the other guys don't.

TIPTON Yeah, but it doesn't bother me. I'm just proud to be part of Judas Priest. If there are guitar polls, you'll never see K.K. or me on top. That's 'cause 50 percent will vote for K. and the other 50 will vote for me. [*laughs*] But really, we sacrifice any selfish egos for the band. All that matters is Judas Priest.

new on the scene—so I don't see them as part of the same wave as Judas Priest. As for rivalry, sure, there was rivalry, because they were trying to claim the throne from us. But in the end, we're all really doing the same thing—trying to encourage fans with the music we all play.

TIPTON In my view, I suppose we were part of a movement, but we were doing things our own way. We were innovative in that respect, but that's not to say we knew the significance of what we were doing at the time; we were just following a form of music that interested us and doing what came naturally. We used to sit in each other's front rooms, playing our guitars in our slippers, and we'd end up writing some classic metal! [*laughs*] We've been very lucky with Priest, 'cause we've always had a special chemistry.

Q: **Has there ever been a point in your career, say during the James Vance trial, when it seemed that the music became larger than what you could control?** —*BRAD HOLLAND*

[*In 1989, the parents of teenagers James Vance and Ray Belknap unsuccessfully sued Judas Priest, claiming subliminal messages allegedly found on the* Stained Class *album provoked the boys to attempt suicide.—Ed.*]

DOWNING Not really. I think what was out of control, if anything, was the legal system. My experience is that most lawyers are quite clever and can argue any point! [*laughs*] Looking back, it was all hocus-pocus. At the end of the day, it all came down to money. People thought we had a lot, and they wanted some. But, as much as I might criticize the system, I'm glad to see that justice prevailed.

DEAR GUITAR HERO

IAN
MACKAYE

OF FUGAZI

Q: I love how Fugazi seamlessly segue from song to song. Are these transitions worked out in practice or do they just happen? —*MIKE AMLAND*

They're natural, though after playing hundreds of shows some songs certainly suggest others that should follow them. It started out as a practice ethic; we would just randomly play through the songs over and over and we got in the habit of hearing cues and going different places from there. We continued that approach primarily because it kept the sets interesting to us but also because it allowed us to respond to circumstances. Fugazi have never used a set list, because some nights are different—different crowd, venue or mood. So having a set piece presented every night seemed unnatural.

Q: Is it frustrating that many people overlook your musical legacy and focus on lifestyle issues and the way in which you've run your business affairs? —*DICKIE SIMMONS*

It's disappointing, because it becomes clear that the way information moves is so biased that once people set you in a place it's very hard to escape. I don't think in terms of labels. My definitions tend to be wide open. A lot of people would probably be surprised by what I consider punk and even more surprised by what I would not consider punk. It has nothing to do with funny hair and multiple piercings and everything to do with someone who's constantly working to maintain the free space where new ideas are possible.

Q: I love your sound. What's your typical guitar/amp setup? —*SKYLAR GUZMAN*

Throughout Fugazi, I've had only two guitars—both SGs I bought for $250—and one amp, a Marshall JCM800 run through a Marshall 4x12. I use no effects. I was always into going as far as I could with just a guitar, a cable and an amp, seeing how many different sounds I could elicit without resorting to pedals, because they were just too complicated. I'm an anti-option person; if I had an endless array of available sounds I'd spend all my time scratching my head. I'd rather turn on an amp and take it from there.

I also don't like the way effects lessen the organic, tactile aspect of playing guitar. With certain effects, you can get the same signal hitting it with all your force or touching it with your pinkie, and I actually look at guitar playing in almost exactly the opposite way. To me, it's all about the touch. I'm not busy figuring out how to dial things up; I'm trying to figure out how to make more interesting sounds with my hands, by altering where I pick, by how heavy my attack is, or by playing with the volume and tone

How do you handle being known as a major influence on a generation of musicians?

—RYAN GERDES

To think about what's it like to be influential requires one to spend time meditating on what one has done. But then you're not "doing"—and I'm interested in doing. Interviews are among the only times I discuss stuff in this way. When I wake up, I'm not thinking about all the people I've influenced. I just do my work.

I will say this: music was never a choice for me; it was just on. I started out loving Jimi Hendrix, the Beatles and Janis Joplin, then became completely obsessed with Ted Nugent and Parliament, among others. Then punk came along and blew my mind. Seeing a band like the Bad Brains in 1979 was just so incredible and overwhelming. Music kicked my ass, and I only intend to return the favor.

controls. I am also endlessly interested in feedback. My single favorite musician is Jimi Hendrix. I love the way he fooled around with feedback, and I am very interested in the atmosphere it can create, how it can be manipulated and how it sounds different on every stage.

 Every moment of Minor Threat footage I've seen astounds me. How did the band keep up that level of intensity for three years?
—*BRIAN BIRCKBICHLER*

We were in the middle of a really explosive musical and cultural renaissance. As teenagers seeing groups like the Bad Brains, Black Flag, the Circle Jerks and D.O.A. there was no way to respond except to play as hard as you could. I have a personal ethic about performance, which is to take every opportunity to go onstage very seriously and with every intention of just destroying and putting everything I have into what I'm doing. That's how the whole band operated.

 Are you horrified by any of the bands that cite you as their godhead?
—*STU JOHNSON*

Not unless they are superviolent fundamentalists or something. While I'm sure I wouldn't count all of these bands as my favorites, and some I wouldn't even find particularly interesting, I'm also sure that a lot of bands I cite as an influence would scratch their heads if they ever heard my music.

DEAR GUITAR HERO

JAKE E. LEE

Q: **Do you receive any royalties from your work with Ozzy, or was everything you did for him covered under your salary?** —*M. SANDS*

I don't receive royalties. For my work on *Bark at the Moon*, I was given options, the best being that I was paid for my songwriting contributions. For *The Ultimate Sin*, I pressed for credit and publishing [*royalties*], which I got, but after being fired I was presented with basically the same options I received for *Bark at the Moon* and decided to sell my share of the publishing. My only real regret is being uncredited for writing most of the music on *Bark at the Moon*.

Q: **At the end of "Bark at the Moon," did you use hammer-ons or pull-offs or a combination of both?** —*SETH FOSTER*

The 16th notes at the end of "Bark at the Moon" employ pull-offs, no hammer-ons and a seven-fret stretch in the second half of the four-measure phrases.

 Q: **Though you were one of the very few guys in the Eighties who wasn't sporting a Floyd Rose, you still had amazing dive-bomb effects. I can clearly remember seeing you reach up and twist the tuning pegs in videos. Did you actually do that in live performances? If so, how was your batting average for getting back to the correct pitch?** —*STAN CULLER*

I started incorporating the faux whammy dives via the tuning pegs after seeing [*country guitarist*] Roy Clark do one at the end of a song on [*the TV variety show*] *Hee Haw* when I was 16 or so. At first, I wasn't very accurate, but as with anything, I improved with practice. By the time I was with Ozzy, I could bring the guitar back to pitch 99 percent of the time.

Q: **Your sweeplike technique where you descend and ascend on the fretboard sounds nothing like a neoclassical arpeggio. How do you perform this and how did you come up with it?** —*ZAK*

I'm not really sure exactly what you're referring to, but I'm guessing an example would be the beginning to the solo of "Slow Down," from *Bark at the Moon*. Back when I was first learning the guitar, I'd listen to and read anything on the subject. I'd scour my dad's *Down Beat* magazines for interviews with jazz guitarists, and in one of the interviews there was a mention of a technique called "circle picking," but there was no explanation of it. I imagined the circle originating from the wrist in order to cover three or four strings with a downstroke, then reversing the string order with an upstroke in order to

I love the classical guitar part in the song "Killer of Giants." Did you take classical lessons? Would you recommend other rock guitarists do so?

—MARCUS M.

I took three or four classical guitar lessons, but the teacher was relentless when it came to what I felt were overly rigid techniques. So I ended up quitting. I've always felt that the more exposure you have to varied music, instruments, techniques and cultures, the more resources you have to draw from. You may never actually use something you've learned, but it will be there if you need it.

play an arpeggio. Years later, someone told me that circle picking was actually a single-string technique, but that's how I came up with the technique that I use to play those particular arpeggios.

Q: **What type of distortion pedal did you use during your time with Ozzy, and did you use the clean boost technique like Randy Rhoads?**
—*KYLE DAMRON*

I knew that Randy used an MXR Distortion Plus, but I didn't know he used it as a clean boost. Yes, the Boss OD-1 that I used during my time with Ozzy was set with the volume maxed and the distortion on minimum. I'd turn it off for the clean parts to regain the bottom end.

Q: **How do you play the beginning part of "Shot in the Dark"?**
—*PAUL DARROCH*

The intro to "Shot in the Dark" employs natural harmonics on the B string at the 12th, 7th and 5th frets and then pressing the string behind the nut. That's followed by a harmonic at the 4th fret on the G string with more behind-the-nut string pressing.

Q: **Around the time that *The Ultimate Sin* came out, I read that you considered using the whammy bar a cop out. How do you feel about it now that guitarists such as Steve Vai have used it to enhance the natural voices of their guitars?** —*RUSS*

I've never looked down on whammy bar use. Jimi Hendrix, Jeff Beck, Adrian Belew and numerous other guitarists have used it inventively and tastefully. I just got tired of hearing a large faction of the newer players at the time dive bomb their way in and out of solos as a cop out.

Q: **You have many unorthodox techniques, including bringing the thumb of your fretting hand around to the front of the neck and using it to fret notes and make superwide stretches that sound like two-handed tapping. When did you come up with that technique and was it for a specific solo or song?** —*JASON RIEDEL*

That started one night when I was living with Warren DeMartini, who was my roommate for a while. We were sitting around playing our guitars, and he started showing me

121

Is it true that George Lynch was going to be Ozzy's guitarist before Ozzy saw you in a club?

—TANNER

George had been tagged to replace Brad Gillis on tour after Randy Rhoads died, and he was actually on tour with them, learning the songs and playing at the soundchecks. Apparently, Ozzy wasn't happy with George's sound and asked Dana Strum, who arranged his auditions, to have [*session guitarist*] Mitch Perry and me audition with him at S.I.R. studios in L.A. Dana called me the night before and said we had to learn "Crazy Train" and "I Don't Know." I wasn't familiar with the songs and had to borrow the album from a friend to learn them. Despite showing up late, not knowing the songs as well as I should have *and* refusing to do an off-the-cuff solo for them, I was offered the gig. Ozzy told me I'd be leaving for England in three days and playing the European gigs in a week.

these wide spacings he could fret because his fingers were so much longer than mine. I didn't want to be outdone, but the only way I could hit the same frets was to use my fretting-hand thumb over the fingerboard. Warren thought that was hilarious, and whenever another guitarist would drop in, he'd say, "Hey, Jake, do that thumb thing for him!" Eventually, I realized I should use the technique to come up with something a little more melodically complex.

Q: **When you bend the neck of your guitar for your dive bomb effect, is that safe? I want to do this live, but I am afraid of snapping off the neck. Is there a trick to it? Does doing this knock the guitar badly out of tune?**
—ANONYMOUS

When I bend the neck, I do it as far from the neck joint as possible, depending on the position of my left hand. Ultimately, you want to hold the neck at the tip of the head-stock with your left hand and grab the upper horn of the body with your right hand. I wouldn't be too concerned about a Fender guitar being able to handle it, but I'd be really careful with a Gibson. And yes, it does tend to knock a guitar out of tune. I try to give the strings a little tweak behind the nut after a big bend, and that usually helps bring it back around. I've gotta say, some of the bends I did when I was performing with Ozzy were so big, I was surprised the neck didn't snap.

Q: **Settle this once and for all: is your white guitar a Fender or a Charvel?**
—ANONYMOUS

It's a 1975 Fender hardtail Stratocaster that I purchased new. It had a sunburst finish, but by 1981 it had become so ratty looking that my roommate, who worked in the Charvel paint room, offered to paint it for free. In the process, he cut down the Fender headstock and slapped a Charvel sticker on it.

DEAR GUITAR HERO

RITCHIE BLACKMORE

Q: **I believe you were the first person to scallop the neck of your guitar. What inspired you to do so, and do you have anything similar done to your acoustic guitars?** —*STEVE ATHEY*

I first did this when I was 18 after playing an old guitar whose neck was so pitted that it had a scalloped effect. I liked it so much that I sandpapered the wood between the frets, and I loved the results. The scallop makes holding a bent note easier because the string does not get caught up. I also find it gives me more control over the vibrato. My acoustics are custom-made by a few small luthiers, and I have had some of the guitars scalloped, though it is less essential on acoustics because, when playing them, I rely on trills more than bends.

Q: **I have long marveled at your ability to keep your Strats in tune, given your style of heavy bending and tremolo dives. Do you have any tips or tricks you could share?** —*J. TODD*

Indeed I do. Leo Fender made Stratocasters with an extreme angle for the tailpiece—it's nearly 45 degrees, I believe—and setting it as such makes all the difference. If done so with the right amount of springs, the trem unit will always return to being perfectly in tune. I didn't believe this until the guy who fixed my guitars showed me. He would correct the action only about once every six months. I called Fender to tell them, and they knew absolutely nothing about it. They just assumed tremolo units went out of tune.

Q: **Does it anger you that Yngwie Malmsteen made the inclusion of classical music into rock look ridiculous?** —*JUSTIN DAVIS*

No, not at all. Yngwie is a very good player. He is much better than people give him credit for. I think his wardrobe might bother me more than his playing.

Q: **I've always loved how the organ and guitar solos meshed in Deep Purple, especially on "Burn." How closely did you and [keyboardist] Jon Lord work out your solos?** —*LEE WANGLE*

We worked very closely, because we generally went into a song understanding we would each take a solo. Generally, we would each write out the progressions we wanted to solo over, and then show them to each other. On "Burn," we sort of swapped solos. I was having a very hard time with the progression I had written myself, but Jon liked it, so he took it over for his solo and I wrote a new one for myself.

You are a virtuoso guitarist, yet you are most associated with "Smoke on the Water," one of the all-time simplest and coolest riffs. Are you surprised that riff has had such a lasting impact?
—CARMEN DAVIS

Yes and no. I am kind of surprised so many people jumped on it, when there are so many other riffs that I think are better, but it pays the bills, so I don't mind. I was trying to write something simple. When I first started writing music, I listened to people like Pete Townshend and marveled at how simple and catchy his music was. I was following that route with "Smoke on the Water." Writing something banal but catchy is an art in itself, one that is often more difficult than writing a complex piece with many parts.

You had such a great rock sound. What were you playing through on *Machine Head*? —*MICHAEL CURRY*

I was using a 200-watt Marshall with a Treble Booster, probably a Hornby Skewe, but I can't say for sure which Strat I was playing. For one thing, I used to change the necks on my guitars often because I might like the feel but not the sound. I also glued necks in place so they couldn't move.

 For such a seemingly simple riff, "Smoke on the Water" is played many different ways. So which method is correct: power chords or single-note passes? —*JOHN PARADIS*

It's played with two notes picked at the same time, using fingers rather than a pick. It sounds wrong when strummed as a chord or picked with all downstrokes. The bass part of the riff is plucked downward with the thumb while the finger is pulling up. I pick the fourth and fifth strings together on the fifth fret, then I pick the third and fourth strings on the third fret. The next shape is on the same two strings on the fifth fret, then the semitone above that, and then back to the first two shapes.

What has been the one thing in your rig that has remained the same through the years? —*SEAN OSTER*

My tape recorder, which I converted into a preamp in '72. We've tried to emulate that sound with a million different pieces of gear, none of which sounded right. So I've continually carted around this big tape recorder that is falling apart. Finally, some German guy made me a little box that seems to replicate the sound; it flattens it and fattens it up without fuzzing it up. That is now my backup and one of these days may actually replace the irreplaceable.

You once categorically stated that "Eric Clapton is not a very good guitar player." Why would you say that, especially since he gave you your first Stratocaster? —*MARLON CORTES*

Those were not my exact words, and I regret that what I said came across as a putdown; that's not how I meant it. Eric is very good, but it's amazing that so many other guitarists are forgotten about or never known. That's the point I was trying to make, that there are a lot of other brilliant guitarists. Eric has done a lot for the guitar, especially with some of his work with Cream, and he certainly did a lot for me by turning me on to Strats as well as Clifford Essex strings.

127

You've just woken up and found yourself in the middle of the 16th century. Who is the first person you want to jam with, and will you be able to find musical currency?

—REMI AUDY

My favorite composer is Tillman Susato, so I would hunt him down in Antwerp in the 1530s. He was a music publisher as well as a musician, so he would have lots of Flemish pageantry-style music. I'm not a good reader so it might be a little tricky to play immediately, but I would pick it up by ear and have a grand old time.

As for him giving me my first Strat—actually, he gave it to his roadie, who sold it to me. And in '68, when Deep Purple supported Cream at the Forum in Los Angeles—with Jimi Hendrix and George Harrison in the first row—I asked Eric backstage what kind of strings he used, because I loved his sound.

 Am I crazy to think that Jimi Hendrix is overrated? His blues-based playing could not hold a candle to your work. —*JAMES HOWARD*

You are not crazy but you are wrong. That said, I understand what you are getting at. Although I loved Hendrix's playing, I could see the limitations. He was the best in terms of the overwhelming feel of his playing, arrangements and riffs, and the way his guitar and voice were as one. But from a technical point of view, it wasn't overwhelming, and I think Robert Fripp thought the same.

I loved listening to Hendrix play because he was an extension of the guitar, and it was amazing how he would just make the thing sing. His was a very different approach, and it really made me pause, because I focused on technical players like Chet Atkins, Les Paul and Speedy Bryant. When Hendrix came along, I thought, What is happening here?

What led you to become fascinated with classical chord progressions and harmonies? Did any particular composers excite you? —*ALAN JONES*

The main composer who inspired me was obviously Bach, who had a rock and roll sound on some of his organ pieces. The guys who turned me onto the concept were the guitarists Joe Moretti and Tony Harvey of Nero and the Gladiators. I saw this unbelievable band at a community center when I was 15 and was blown away. They did "In the Hall of the Mountain King" and other classical pieces, and it really grabbed me. I started fiddling with classical pieces right then.

Did any of you guys ever kick Frank Zappa's ass for running away from the fire in Switzerland [*recounted in the lyrics of "Smoke on the Water"*]? —*AMPLE AL*

No, we didn't. Though it was funny how he told the audience to calm down then proceeded to jump out the window.

DEAR GUITAR HERO

JERRY CANTRELL

OF ALICE IN CHAINS

No matter what I try—and I have tried a lot of things—I cannot match your wah sound on "Man in the Box." What kind of pedal did you use to get that elusive sound? —*JAMES BYRNE*

It's just a Dunlop Cry Baby, but the secret is that it's mixed with the signal from a Talk Box, and [*producer*] Dave Jerden did a really nice job blending the two. A Talk Box can sound a little thin or weak on its own, but that riff from "Man in the Box" still sounds great today.

 You have a great tone. What are some of your gear secrets? —*ERIC HAMILTON*

I think tone really is in your hands. My tone comes from the way I grip the neck and hold my fairly thick Tortex pick—choked up quite a bit to get that compressed, stinging sound. Years ago, when we opened for Van Halen, Ed came out and played through my setup, and it sounded like fucking Ed because that tone is in him, not the equipment. The equipment you choose certainly enhances your sound, but really, it's all about flesh and blood.

 It's difficult to pick out your influences when I hear your playing. Who are your biggest heroes? —*JOHN COSTELLO*

Angus and Malcolm Young are number one, because AC/DC are the ultimate rock and roll band. I also love Jimmy Page and Tony Iommi, who as a guitarist probably shined through for me more than anyone. And I was really into Dave Gilmour's phrasing, which is not super pyrotechnic but is chockfull of feeling.

 When are we going to hear some unreleased Alice in Chains material? —*JON CYR*

I don't believe there is much unreleased studio stuff—perhaps a few outtakes. We never went in to make a record with 30 tunes. The European market always wanted extra singles and B-sides, and we thought that was a bunch of crap. Our attitude was, You get what everyone else gets. As soon as CDs came out, albums got bloated, and I'm proud that we didn't succumb to that. There are plenty of live Alice in Chains performances, like the BBC sessions, and they rock pretty hard, but there are no plans to put that stuff out, as far as I know.

PHOTO BY JIMMY HUBBARD

Q: Godsmack is virtually an Alice in Chains tribute band. Does that make you proud or angry? —*CHRIS BEESE*

I think Layne's families should get royalties from the sun design in Godsmack's logo. But aside from that, I'm glad they've had success, and they don't sound like Alice in Chains to me. If people hear that, maybe it's true, which only means we accomplished our goal of creating a smoking band with its own voice and sound. We were a great example of a rock band, for better and worse. Rock bands usually explode, and that's what we did. I certainly wish Layne was still around and we were still playing, but that shit went down and you deal with it. I am too proud of what we accomplished to be sad.

Q: *Dirt* is an amazing heavy album that comes from a very low place. Was it the result of a personal feeling or an artistic projection?
—*JAMES KRIEGER*

Dirt still stings when I listen to it, but in a good way. We wrote about a lot of dark and heavy stuff, but we weren't wallowing in it. For us, it was all about fighting through it, triumphing and taking it to the limit—going to the wall and breaking through it. That's still the place I try to write from. There's enough fluff out there; I want something that means something, written by a real person who's lived a real life.

Q: Alice in Chains was a glam band in its earliest days. What led to your transition? —*JOE MCGREEDY*

We were all kids, coming out of the decade of Guns N' Roses and hair metal. Everyone starts somewhere, and we were lucky enough to find ourselves as a band before we put our first record out. The glam inspiration was just a result of the times we were living in, and we have no reason to regret it.

Q: I always loved your solo in "Dam That River." Was it written out or improvised? —*LISA RICE*

It's total agro but I constructed it. We had very little time and money to make *Dirt*, so we had that shit worked out. Our producers, Dave Jerden and Toby Wright, both freaked at the way I doubled or tripled my tracks by just listening to the bass and drums and not my original track. On *Dirt* we even went to three tracks on each side—low-, mid- and high-frequency tracks. I never listened to any of them during the overdubs, but that shit is pretty damn spot on.

You guys were always lumped in with grunge bands. How connected did you feel to Pearl Jam, Soundgarden and Nirvana?

—WAYNE GARCIA

When we first started out, everyone from those bands thumbed their noses at us because we were not a Sub Pop band. The local press vehemently attacked us for that. But we actually jumped out of the gate first; we were the first to go Gold and the first to do arena tours because we would play with anybody, from Extreme to Slayer. We would take any gig, and it served us well and helped the other bands. Soundgarden cracked the door, we kicked it open, and Nirvana and Pearl Jam blew it off the hinges. All that being said, we were all really tight and very supportive of each other. I am still amazed by the quality and individuality of all the bands. It was a beautiful moment in time.

Why have you had a second guitarist on all your solo shows after being the sole guitar player in AIC? —*MARC SCHNEIDER*

When I play live, the vocals are my main focus. I figured that if I was going to have a vocalist there to help with harmonies, I might as well get a singer who can play guitar, too. And since this was my first time onstage as a lead vocalist, I wanted extra support all the way around.

 I always felt your harmonies were one of Alice's secret weapons. Your voice is so similar to Layne's. Was that a coincidence or did you work to match his voice? —*JERRY EMBERS*

It was just a result of who I am, and fortunately the blend of our voices was such a unique sound, and it's something I'm really proud of. But I still wouldn't say it's a coincidence. We made records together since 1990 and we worked hard on getting a really good sound in every area.

 You and Layne wrote almost all the songs on the first two albums. Why was *Jar of Flies* more of a full-band effort? —*FRAN TALOTTA*

The other guys wanted to write more. So after a vacation, when we were heading into the studio to record an EP, I decided not to write anything and give everyone else more room to contribute. We got to the studio and everyone wanted to know what I had. When I said "nothing" they thought I was joking. Then we all panicked because we had seven days of studio time and no songs. Mike had some great ideas that I started helping arrange into songs. I had some riffs, which we started layering, and Layne started writing the vocals. And it came together. That's creativity at its finest. We walked in with nothing and walked out with *Jar of Flies* seven days later.

Is it true that all of your solos on *Dirt* were cut as scratch takes? —*BRYAN CADENA*

[*laughs*] No, no. That's only true of one song, "Hate to Feel," which was a joke lead—just me making a lot of noise to fill the space. When I went back to redo it, Mike and Layne wouldn't let me, and they were right. Every solo on *Dirt* is prime, smoking shit. A lot of them were first takes, however.

DEAR GUITAR HERO

ROBBY KRIEGER

OF THE DOORS

Q: **Is it true that you'd been playing guitar for only six months when you joined the Doors? How did you grasp the instrument's vocabulary so quickly?** —*EDDIE ROY*

Actually, I had been playing *electric* guitar for just six months when I joined the group; I'd been playing folk and flamenco acoustic for three or four years before then. When I started to play the electric, I just used the same fingerpicking style that I used on the acoustic. That's the only method that I used when I played with the Doors, but about 20 years ago I learned to use a pick for playing speedier runs. Now I'm half and half.

Q: **Have you ever thought of creating an alter ego with an anagram of your name, as Jim did with Mr. Mojo Risin? You could be Reb Kirby Gore, if you want to become a rabbi. Or, if you buy a motorcycle, you could be Biker Rob Grey!** —*ANTHONY JONES*

I never thought of that. Those are pretty good. Thank you, Anthony.

Q: **Why did you have such an affinity for the Gibson SG?** —*ACE*

I wanted a big red Gibson, like [the ES-335] Chuck Berry used to play, but I could only afford a Melody Maker, which—at 200 bucks—seemed close enough. I used it on the first Doors album, and then I got an SG.

Q: **I love your solo in "When the Music's Over." Which scale did you use, and what effect gives it that great distortion?** —*THIAGO RAVACHE*

There is no scale; the whole point of that solo was to not use a scale. I tried to play like John Coltrane and just go as far out as possible. It's actually two guitars: we recorded four tracks and then picked the pair that intertwined the best. Paul got that fuzz violin–type sound by sticking a little resistor in the board.

Q: **I love the composition of "Peace Frog," which features many sections, including a great bridge. Were the parts written all at once? And how did you get that great tone for the solo?** —*RICHARD TRELLES*

I wrote the basic form for the music and breaks. They were then given the "Doors" treatment by the three of us and Harvey Brooks, who was playing bass. We recorded the track before the lyrics were written, which is not how we normally did things. We cut it, and then Jim and [*producer*] Paul Rothchild went through Jim's poetry books and found

Jim never seemed to change his leather pants. Did they smell?

—AL HUNTER

I never got close enough to find out, but they were capable of standing up by themselves.

a poem called "Abortion Story," which had all the stuff about "blood in the streets." The two of them came up with a vocal line to fit the music. As far as the sound on the solo, I used a Twin Reverb turned up really loud. The echo was created with a tape delay. At the time, there wasn't a pedal that could create that effect.

Q: **You've said that Jim was funnier than people realize. Could you describe a typical joke of his?** —*CHUCK SHOWALTER*

In the early days when we were all taking a lot of acid, we were at a party, and this guy who had just dropped a ton of the stuff showed up. Jim started flicking the lights off and on really fast. Actually, the guy freaked out pretty bad. But it *was* funny.

Q: **The best questions must be those that none of us have enough knowledge to ask. How about telling us a Doors anecdote to a question you haven't been asked yet?** —*JEFF KELLY*

Unfortunately, all the questions have been asked.

DEAR GUITAR HERO

JOE
SATRIANI

Q: **How do you pull off those amazing dive bombs that go up instead of down? For instance, in "Satch Boogie" you go up almost five half steps, just before the solo starts.** *—KEVIN LAND*

You start by stimulating the artificial harmonic on the G string, in the area between the two pickups. Then, you quickly depress the bar with your *fret* hand and gradually bring it up, until the note heard is just above the pitch of the note that was originally sounded. That's what creates the illusion that you've started at the note and dramatically raised the pitch. I perform this a little differently every night. I purposely improvise it because I would go insane playing it precisely the same night after night.

 Q: **Guitar heroes are famous for their big egos. Is that why your guitar looks like a mirror?** *—ANONYMOUS*

Actually, the guitar reflects the audience, not the player.

Q: **Who do you think got the most out of your teachings: Kirk Hammett or Steve Vai?** *—NORMAN S.*

I'd have to say Steve did, because he was a complete beginner when he started, and Kirk was already playing in Exodus. Steve and I started at the very beginning: "This is an E chord."

Q: **Why have you remained so faithful to Ibanez guitars?** *—NICK PAYNE*

They make the best guitar for me and have included every little thing I've requested in the design of the JS line. That includes wood composition, pickups, frets, neck radius, paint jobs and so on. There aren't many guitars that allow me to play the oldest and newest styles, which is what I need to do every night. You can't do that with a vintage Telecaster or a reissue Les Paul, great as they are in their own right.

Q: **Your head and your guitars are very shiny. Do you use the same compound to make them sparkle?** *—PAT MCILVEEN*

Of course: Joe's Special Chrome Dome Polish.

 Q: **Where do you get your oh-so-cool hats?** *—EVAN HOROWITZ*

Finally, an important question! They are made by Project Alabama, a collective of Alabaman women who sew. I haven't gotten used to having a shaved head so I prefer to wear a hat at all times, but you have to be careful not to wear anything too tight, because it will

When you jam, do you think in modes and tonalities or do you just play?

—ACE COMPARATO

There's a moment prior to jamming when I review in my mind what the musicians and I are going to do. At that point, it's hard to stop myself from thinking, Wouldn't it be clever to try and superimpose this mode over that one? But once I start playing, I'm not thinking at all. I'm sure there are some background programs going on in my brain, because when you know music theory it becomes the method your sub-conscious uses to guide you. Steve Vai is the same way. When we jam during the G3 show, standing back to back, we're each doing everything we can to play something new or to complement one another in an unexpected way. We're reacting to one another, rather than thinking about what we should be playing. We're able to do that because the thinking has already been done; it's so ingrained in us that it frees us to just play.

leave a line on your head. When you have hair you worry about hat hair, and when you don't you worry about hideous red rings. The hats I wear are light cotton and always feel good.

I actually have a long history of wearing silly hats and clothing. In fact, the very first time I was pictured in *Guitar World*, I was wearing an absurd silver vest that looked like it came out of Sonny Bono's closet. I've always tried to poke fun at how rock stars are supposed to look.

Q: **Do you have a regular warmup routine?** —*BRENDA JOHNSON*
I like playing simple songs with different chords and running through chromatic exercises grouped in twos, threes and fours, which I put in my *Guitar Secrets* book. I also do hammer-ons, pull-offs and things like that for 15 to 20 minutes before playing actual parts, which require that I be ready to play anything.

Q: **Technology has made the editing process easier, but has knowing you can re-edit and shuffle parts around changed the way you approach playing? And is there anything technologically that still frustrates you as a player?** —*SCOTT CONNER*
I think the advent of Pro Tools and Logic Audio takes some anxiety out of recording. But remember this: prior to digital recording, you could always do 100 takes and use the best parts of each by splicing them together. It was more tedious, but people have been doing it that way forever. Still, I think digital technology has made it easier to fix things, and that helps to eliminate the "red light fever" that goes with studio recording—the anxiety that comes with knowing you're recording. In that respect, I think it has really freed up drummers because they have so much pressure to nail a song from beginning to end.

The most frustrating thing about digital recording is the anxiety that the system will bomb and there won't be anything there. The technology is still iffy, and if you lose something you can spend as much money trying to retrieve it as you've spent on everything else up to that point. As a result, many of us back up our digital recordings to two-inch recording tape. For instance, *Engines of Creation* was 100 percent digitally created but all of the mixes were done on analog tape. It sounds backward, but it's still the best way to guarantee that you'll have reliable copies around.

Q: **Have you read any issues from the latest *Silver Surfer* series?** —*C. NELSON*
No. I don't follow the Silver Surfer at all. Odd as it seems, I've never been much into comics.

DEAR GUITAR HERO

MICK
MARS

OF MÖTLEY CRÜE

Q: I heard that when you were in the studio for *Dr. Feelgood*, you used so many amps that your guitar leaked onto the Aerosmith album being recorded in the same building [*1989's* Pump]. Is this true? —*JUSTIN HACHEY*

That's right. Steven Tyler was doing vocals with producer Bruce Fairbairn next door, and I remember them yelling at me, "You've gotta turn your stuff down, Mick! It's leaking into our vocals." I didn't turn down, though. I just told them, "Hey, that's the way I play—loud." [*laughs*] So yeah, I'm all over the record they were doing. Somewhere in the mix, you'll hear me.

Q: I've always seen you as a mellow character, and I just want to know, what's the secret to surviving 30 years of Nikki Sixx, Vince Neil and Tommy Lee? —*JUSTIN MICHAEL HUGHES*

I have my own bus! [*laughs*] Personal space—my own bus, my own hotel room, my own dressing room, my own private time... That's the secret. A lot of times, the rest of the guys will fly from one gig to the next. It takes them an hour to go from one city to another, whereas it might take me a day and a half on the bus. But the payoff is I'm rested, I'm in a good place mentally, and nobody's driven me crazy. [*laughs*] In the early days, I couldn't do that, so I had to deal with Nikki blasting his music all the time, Tommy running around with no clothes on, Vince doing whatever he was doing...all sorts of behavior. I'm glad to travel with a little sanity now.

Q: Like you, I've had ankylosing spondylitis [*a.k.a. AS, an inflammatory form of arthritis Mars has battled since age 19*] since my early twenties. It's tough, I but gotta keep going. I'm wondering this: do you approach the instrument and performing differently than before the disease really took hold? Any advice for guitarists with health challenges? —*CHARLES POTTER*

My approach hasn't changed, really. My posture, yes; my playing, no. AS gets into your hands, wrists, feet, your ankles. It rarely, rarely gets anywhere else, like into your spine, but in my case, yes, it did spread there. My case is pretty severe in that it's traveled all the way up to my brain stem. My posture has changed pretty drastically. I've shrunk about five inches. There's a way I could've not shrunk, and that would've been to lay flat when sleeping. The only problem with that, though, would be that I couldn't look down at my guitar—I'd be standing totally straight and unable to bend my neck. Luckily, the doctors didn't tell me this, so I'm kind of bent now, a little hunched over, but at least I

It's been well documented, often by all the other guys in the band, that Mötley Crüe epitomized Eighties rock decadence. As the one guy in the band who's had his head on straight, what stands out for you as the craziest moment on the road?

—JON RUBIN

I don't know. They've all been crazy! [*laughs*] I guess it depends on what era and what tour—there's been different levels to Mötley's craziness. One thing that stands out in my mind is the night in Vegas when everybody in the band got arrested, except me. The rest of the guys were pushing cops around, but I had the sense not to get involved. I had already been in jail once when I was a teenager, and no way was I going to go back. Getting into fights with cops? That's pretty bad. I knew that was only going to lead to big-time trouble. I told the guys, "Don't do it. Don't go messin' with cops." They didn't listen. I'll tell you, so much of being on tour is kind of a haze. Getting drunk, doing drugs, falling off the stage—sure, I've done all of that. But I always kept playing, no matter what.

can look down at my guitar when I play. AS hurts, but I don't use steroids or anything like that. Sometimes I have really good days, sometimes I don't.

My advice would be this: don't take the quick fix. Don't just go to a doctor and start taking all the drugs he pushes on you. I got hooked on pills and didn't play guitar for two years. Play through the pain if you can.

 Out of all your recordings with Mötley Crüe, which guitar solo is your personal favorite, and why? —*BLAKE BURLESON*

Probably the solo on the song "Primal Scream" [*from 1991's* Decade of Decadence], because it's very bluesy and it's a lot of fun for me to play. The solo just screams the blues. I put a lot of different guitar players' styles in it, everyone from Jimmy Page to Johnny Winter to Michael Bloomfield. I took all of those influences and used them to create that solo.

Have you ever thought about releasing a solo album? —*LARRY KELLY*

Yes. I'm working on some things right now. I probably have about seven or eight songs, but I'm not totally happy with them yet. I want to go in a totally different direction from Mötley. Not in some weird and wacky way that will alienate friends and family and fans, but more in the way that Hendrix did *Electric Ladyland*, the Beatles did *Sgt. Pepper's* and the Beach Boys did *Pet Sounds*. Those records were still them, but they were really removed from what those artists had done before. You went, "Wow! Now that's a record." The [*Beatles'*] White Album—that's where I'm going. I'm not saying I'm going to play like them, but I want to do something...see, I don't want to use the word *landmark*, because people will think that's really stupid and egotistical. But I want people to say, "Wow! I didn't know Mick Mars could do that." Think Eric Clapton with the *Layla* album or Hendrix with *Electric Ladyland*...something you can listen to for hours.

DEAR GUITAR HERO

JOHN
PETRUCCI

OF DREAM THEATER

Q: I've been a longtime Dream Theater fan, but always felt your 2003 album, *Train of Thought*, brought things to a new level for the band. What did you do differently with that album? —*JASON A. KING*

Thanks. We wrote the two albums before that one in the studio, and recorded the songs as soon as we finished writing them. With *Train*, we went back to holding writing sessions and rehearsal periods where we cranked up the amps and let it rip, rather than sit there with headphones and worry about our parts. That helped us craft more dramatic, less-experimental material, the kind of stuff that's always the most fun to play live and which crowds respond to best. I wanted every song to have that energy. We also tried not to overrecord and keep the arrangements cleaner so there was more breathing room in the songs. Guitarwise, I wanted to have more intense soloing and over-the-top parts while keeping the songs structured and melodic and lyrically strong.

 Q: If you could be any superhero, who would you be and why? —*JOSH CATLETT*

Superman, because I like the way he could fly around the earth and turn back time. I want more practice time!

 Q: How do you do those awesome high-to-low sweeps in "Under a Glass Moon"? —*DAVE SCARBOROUGH*

I focus on two elements to make those sound good. First, I really separate the notes with my fretting hand so they don't ring out like a chord. I use some alternate chord shapes that help with this. Second, I drag the pick from one string to the next using the hand's momentum. That way, I'm not actually picking the individual strings but rather pulling the pick up against the string.

Q: What do you use to get that great, distinct distortion sound? And do you have any thoughts on acoustic simulation gear? —*RUSS ADDISON*

My distortion usually comes from the amp. On *Train of Thought*, I used a Mesa/Boogie Road King, which has a very cool liquidy overdrive that also lends itself to clarity and separation of notes. For acoustic simulation, the Fishman piezo system in my Music Man signature guitar sounds so good that I've recorded with it. It's very convenient and allows you to switch back and forth and blend sounds.

Let's cut to the chase: how can I improve my speed?

—MAX PIGAULT

There are a few different ways. First is the tried-and-true metronome method, in which you play a phrase slowly 10 times, then increase the metronome's speed and play it 10 times again, and so on. The key is to make sure you can play the part at speed before moving on to the next level. The second method is to simply practice a lick over and over at varying speeds, without ever stopping. The third way is to break a lick into tiny fragments and master each at a high speed until you have the whole thing down pat.

Did being a guitar teacher affect your playing? And what do you feel makes a person a good guitar teacher? —*JOHN STRANGE*

Yes, it did affect my playing. It forced me to stay on top of my musical theory and learn songs and techniques that I wasn't interested in, but which my students wanted to learn. A good guitar teacher will create an individual plan for each student rather than expect everyone to fall into his overall method.

 Most guitarists go through a phase of learning other people's material note for note. What did you master this way, and do you still do it now that your playing has reached such a high level? —*WOUTER ECTORS*

Of course I did it. I learned by figuring out stuff like Steve Morse's "Introduction," the Dixie Dregs' "The Bash," Randy Rhoads' solo on "Over the Mountain" and tons of stuff by Yngwie, Al Di Meola, Allan Holdsworth, Steve Vai and Joe Satriani. Working on other people's solos always gives you fresh perspectives and develops your ear, which is why I still do it. It's always good to challenge yourself. That way you don't get to a point where you've learned enough and say, "That's it."

 Does [*Dream Theater bassist*] John Myung ever talk? —*ANONYMOUS*

I understand your confusion; to most people John is certainly a man of few words, but I've known him my whole life and we've had some of the lengthiest, deepest conversations I've ever had with anyone.

PAUL
STANLEY

OF KISS

You have stated in the past that the Kiss guitar sound is basically two guitars that sound like one big one. Can you expand on that? —*JIM*

I remember going to see Humble Pie and loving how the guitar work of Steve Marriott and Peter Frampton, and later, Clem Clempson, melded into one big guitar sound. It doesn't mean playing in unison or playing the same chord formation; it's more like having two different voicings playing against one another and creating a chord that couldn't be produced by one guitarist alone.

 If you could play only one guitar for the rest of your life, what would it be? —*B.C. BONES*

Wow. That's a tough one. My roots are in vintage guitars, and at this point I want a guitar that has a vintage feel but also feels like it's always been mine. I've always thought that guitar players, at least rock players, are pretty much divided between the Fender and the Gibson schools. In that sense, I've always been a Gibson man, but my guitar doesn't have to be a Gibson, as long as it embodies the same features.

 You've written so many classic songs. Can you pick one that you felt never lived up to the rest of the record and explain why? —*DAVE STREUD*

I never felt that at the time I wrote a song. But in hindsight, there are some songs that I listen to and think, This is not great. There have definitely been periods where Kiss' music has lost some of its direction or focus. Some of our songs from the Eighties don't hold up. An album like *Carnival of Souls*, to me, is a mistake of at least the magnitude of [*Music From*] *The Elder*. That's because *Carnival of Souls* was—not of my design, mind you—an attempt to be current or competitive with a style of music that we weren't a part of. It fell flat for that reason. That's not to say that it wasn't a good album, just that it had nothing to do with Kiss. Some of our songs from the Eighties were shallow. They just don't have the depth or the foundation of our other songs.

 Do you ever feel competitive with other guitar players or feel you have something to prove? —*DON CRUTCHFIELD*

Do I feel competitive? Oh gosh, no. I've spent the better part of 40 years playing guitar, really honing what I do. Are there people who play faster? Sure. Are there people who know more chords? Sure, but that's never been what I've been about. My goal is to be a guitar player who can pretty much handle anything—someone who can hold down the

fort. To me, that's a guitar player's most important role. There are some really flashy lead guys around who couldn't play a solid rhythm with a gun to their head. [*laughs*] But no, I never feel competitive. I'd feel totally comfortable getting up and playing with anybody.

Q: I've heard that the long-term plan for Kiss is to get to a point where even you and Gene don't have to be onstage anymore. Is there any truth to that, and can Kiss exist without any of the four original members? —*JOHN ESTEP*

Well, the only part I take exception to in your question is the idea that we wouldn't "have" to be onstage. I think it's more that we might not *belong* onstage. We may reach a point where Kiss may be better off, and the fans may be better served, without us. The goal, as time goes on, is to be able to separate ourselves from what we created and still have it live on. Practically speaking, eventually our choice will be to do that or call it quits. I think that Kiss, loved or hated, has been a source of inspiration or irritation for as long as I can remember. And I'm proud of it.

Q: Have you watched *Gene Simmons Family Jewels*? You're much more private than Gene. Could you ever see cameras in your house following you around? —*CHAD SMITHFIELD*

No, I haven't watched it. It has no appeal to me, whatsoever. Any attempt to film a reality program—whether it's a pseudo–reality show or an actual reality show—is going to make the situation itself unreal, just by nature of having cameras present. And no, I couldn't imagine it for myself. I'd rather have bamboo slivers put under my nails. To me, your sanity comes from your privacy. It's something sacred and all your own.

Q: In the early days of Kiss, before you hit it big, what tactics helped you get through the rough spots? —*STEVE LOTT*

Believing that I was right. You have to believe in yourself, because if you don't, who else will? And you always gotta meet the opposition with twice the force that they meet you.

JEFF
HANNEMAN

OF SLAYER

If you were to go on a real-life *Call of Duty*–style killing spree, what album would you pick as the soundtrack? —*HARRY REAGAN*

It would have to be *Reign in Blood*, obviously. It's relentless all the way through. Twenty-eight minutes and I'd be done. [*laughs*]

 You seem to keep pretty private, while Kerry seems to be everywhere. What do you do when you're not on "Slayer time"? —*ROB WELLS*

I hang with my woman, and with some friends that have nothing to do with Slayer. I also like to watch sports and go to hockey and football games.

 You've mentioned in the past that you record stuff that you don't use with Slayer. What does it sound like, and do you plan to do anything with it in the future. —*MIKA JAAKONAHO*

Every now and then I write something that at the time I feel is not right for Slayer. Then years go by and I find it again, and I'm like, This is *cool*. Some of the stuff from *Seasons in the Abyss* I wrote years before we recorded that album. I'll bring out these old ideas and play them for the guys, and they're like, "Fuck, let's use it." I have a method of working on music: I'll get up in the morning and throw down some drums on my drum machine, and then I'll come back later and try to pop off rhythms to it. Some of it's cool but too tacky or too melodic or something for Slayer. I'll probably do something with it after Slayer decides to quit, but I can't see doing a side project.

 You're one of the fastest right-hand pickers in thrash. How can I increase my speed and endurance? —*MARK KRAMER*

I've been asked this question before, and the only thing I can say is that Kerry and I warm up a lot before we go on. We start, like, an hour before so we can build up our speed in time for the set.

 Lots of people I know form bands in hopes of getting girls. But I'm in a metal band in Ohio, and it doesn't seem to be the case. When you first started Slayer, did it help you score with chicks? —*ANTAR TURGAY*

Not at all. [*laughs*] The majority of our fans are dudes. And the chicks you do see at our shows are probably there because of a dude. Slayer shows are nothing but sausage fests. [*laughs*] We always joke that we really need to write some love songs or something.

Who would you rather share a beer with, Jimi Hendrix or John Lennon, and why?

—JOHN MCNEIL

I'd say Jimi Hendrix, because I'd like to see what was going on in his head. He had no rules on the guitar, and I'd really like to see what's going on upstairs.

Q: **What's the least metal tune we would find on your iPod?** —*AAZAN HABIB*

Probably B-52s. [*laughs*] I like to go hang at the beach or the pool, and they're kind of the perfect music for that.

Q: **What is the scariest thing you've seen a fan do at a Slayer show?**
—*ALONSO LOAIZA*

Every now and then they get too crazy and headbang on the ground or on the barrier, and knock themselves out. At a recent show, I looked down into the pit and there was this guy just lying there, and he looked totally dead. He might have just passed out from exhaustion, but I never found out.

Q: **Do you believe in a spiritual plane, like Satan, God or aliens? Or is this world the only thing out there?** —*"GENGHIS" CONNORS*

I'm pretty much an atheist, so I'd say this world is the only thing we got.

LESLIE WEST

Q: **Did you ever play with Eddie Van Halen, who says he's one of your biggest fans?** —*COREY DECAMP*

Eddie Van Halen got me playing the guitar again. When I was in rehab in Milwaukee, back in 1976, Van Halen were on their first tour, opening for Journey and Montrose. I hadn't gone to any shows in a long time. I wasn't playing the guitar at all. I didn't want to *see* a guitar, because I was in really fucked-up, bad shape. I was just getting myself back to where I wanted to go to a show, and Ronnie Montrose said to me, "You've got to see this kid. He plays a Bach organ fugue on the guitar!"

At the time, there was nothing happening to make me want to play. But I heard him playing some stuff, and he has that [*plays "You Really Got Me," Van Halen–style*]. I never heard that song like that! After the show, I went up to Eddie and said, "Man, you make me want to play the guitar again." One day, out of the blue, two Peavey 5150 stacks showed up at my house, along with one of Eddie's Wolfgang guitars!

So we became friends and have stayed friends for a long time. Hearing him gave me such a thrill, and, still to this day, there's nothing like him.

Q: **What is the story of your involvement in the Who's *Who's Next* recording sessions?** —*GENE OSSO*

At the time [*1971*], we were represented by Track Records in England, which was run by the Who's manager, Kit Lambert. Both bands [*Mountain and the Who*] were recording at the Record Plant in New York City, and Kit said to me, "Pete [*Townshend*] would like you to play some lead." I said, "Why? He's the guitar player!" Kit said, "Pete doesn't want to overdub." Then he asked, "Does Felix [*Pappalardi, Mountain's bassist*] play keyboards?" So I said that he'd played some bass and viola on the Cream records. I was real nervous and freaked out, and of course I didn't know the sessions would turn out to be *Who's Next*.

For some reason, Felix thought he was going to play bass, so he had his whole bass rig set up in their studio. When [*the Who bassist John*] Entwistle saw Felix's bass rig, he said "What's this?! I'm the fucking bass player in the Who!" Townshend said to Felix, "We thought you were Felix *Cavaliere* from the Rascals!" Now I was really embarrassed! So Felix, the big Cream producer, leaves, but before he left, he said to me, "Are you okay? Are you in tune?" And I said, "Yeah, I'm in tune!"

So Pete takes us up to the sixth floor where we listen to his demos for "Won't Get Fooled Again," "Behind Blue Eyes" and "Baby Don't You Do It." We start recording,

and I'm playing lead through a 50-watt Marshall plugged into a custom-made Sunn 1x12 bottom, while Pete was using a Hiwatt. During one of the takes, Pete said, "Wait a minute...I want to be the loudest!" I ended up giving Pete a Les Paul Junior after the sessions.

We'd been recording with Jack Douglas, but they went back to England and redid the record with Glyn Johns. It was too bad, especially on "Baby Don't You Do It," with me on the right and Townshend's rhythm on the left. In 1995, *Who's Next* was rereleased with bonus tracks of the stuff I did with them, so I was very happy when that stuff finally came out.

Q: **What inspired Mountain to record the Jack Bruce song "Theme for an Imaginary Western"?** —*ANDREW GORDON*

Jack told me that Eric [*Clapton*] didn't want to do it because it wasn't blues-based; it was a complicated song. Felix heard it when he produced Jack's solo album, *Songs for a Tailor*, and we recorded it in A; I do it in G now. When Felix asked me to solo on it, I right away went to the barre position of A [*plays A minor pentatonic in fifth position*], and he said, "No, no, no!" He told me that every key has a relative minor; he said, "For A, the relative minor is F♯ minor, so pretend you are playing a blues in F♯ minor, and it'll fit over this chord progression!" When I did it, I said, "Holy shit. It fits!"

After I did the solo, I went home and figured out every relative minor key to every major chord! That changed my whole life.

Q: **Why did the original Mountain break up in 1972?** —*TRAVIS GUBERNICK*

Drugs. Felix had a heroin problem, and I had one, too. He didn't want to go out on the road anymore; he'd already made his million dollars, but I hadn't made mine yet. We played our very last show at the Montreal Forum on New Year's Eve. At the time, I didn't want to quit, but Felix did. Things weren't so copasetic in the group, especially with Felix's wife [*Gail Collins*], who ended up shooting and killing him. [*Collins was convicted of criminally negligent homicide after shooting Pappalardi in their Manhattan apartment in 1983.*]

When we went to England, Felix took us all over to Jack Bruce's house, and while Felix was down in the kitchen, Jack and I were upstairs jamming together. Later on, I knew Felix was leaving the band, so I said to Corky [*Laing, Mountain's drummer*], "We've got to fly to England and put a group together." My choices were Chris Stainton on keyboards, plus a bass player, and maybe Joe Cocker on vocals...or, make one call to Jack Bruce!

Is it true that you were the cause of the 1965 New York City blackout?

—JON DIAZ

No, but I'll tell you what happened. I was auditioning with my first group, the Vagrants, at Scott Muni's Rolling Stone Discotheque on 48th Street. The lead singer was hooking up the P.A., which was a shitty little Bogen amp with two columns, and as soon as he plugged it in, the place went black. I walked out on Second Avenue, and I said, "Jesus Christ, the whole street is black. What the hell happened?" But it was a coincidence that it happened just at that moment when he plugged it in. I said, "This must be some fucking powerful amp! For $100 down on Canal Street, wow!"

The whole city went black, so we didn't get to play. We were waiting to see if the power would come back on, and after five hours, I walked up to Scott Muni and I said, "Are we getting paid for this?" He said, "Paid?!"

We were in a hotel room with my manager, so I went in the bathroom to call [*Bruce*]. I said, "Jack, it's Leslie West," and he said, "Oh, hey man." He was playing with [*drummer*] Jon Hiseman at the time. I said, "Do you want to start a group?" and he said, "Yeah!" I said, "Really!" He asked me who the drummer would be, and I suggest Corky, who Jack didn't really know.

After he came back from Germany, we went to Island Studios and recorded a demo of Cream songs. [*Columbia Records producer*] Clive Davis came to see us—West, Bruce and Laing—play at Carnegie Hall, where we sold out two shows and didn't even have an album yet. After we got signed, we went into the studio and did our first record, *Why Dontcha*. Jack was the best musician I ever played with, and I don't think I will find a better one.

GARY
MOORE

Your guitar work on Thin Lizzy's *Black Rose* was extremely influential to me. Please describe your working relationship with Phil Lynott.

—JOSEPH MCKAGAN

I met Phil when I was 16 and we were in a band called Skid Row. He didn't play bass at the time; he was just the singer, and he got fired because he couldn't sing. After that, Phil and I worked together off and on. We had a love-hate thing; we couldn't work together for long periods. For example, my first stint in Thin Lizzy lasted only four months. Still, together we had a good creative spirit. We had a lot of common musical ground, from blues to Celtic music, and it helped us come up with good songs. We worked together closely on the *Black Rose* material; I was practically his right-hand man. I wrote a big part of "My Sarah" and we wrote much of the title track together. I came up with a lot of the melodic ideas and brought in the Celtic aspects.

 What was your relationship with Randy Rhoads and how did he inspire you? —*TANNER REGINA*

He wasn't really an influence on my playing, though I thought he was very impressive. In 1980, Ozzy and I were both living in L.A. and he kept trying to get me to be his guitarist, but I was forming G-Force. I helped him a bit with getting his band together, and by the time he was ready, I was back in London. When they came to England, I met Randy and we became friendly. He'd heard more of my work than I had his because he hadn't even recorded with Ozzy yet. He was very complimentary to me, and I think his playing on "Mr. Crowley" was a little influenced by my work on "Parisienne Walkways."

Ozzy called me the day after Randy was killed and asked me to complete the tour with him. I said yes out of respect for Randy, though it would have been an extremely difficult situation. But before it happened, I fell and chipped a bone in my wrist and was unable to play.

 You recorded *Still Got the Blues* with three blues titans: Albert King, Albert Collins and B.B. King. How were they to work with?

—JEFF GOODMAN

When I did *Still Got the Blues*, I assumed Albert King, one of my first and greatest guitar heroes, would say no, but much to my pleasure and surprise, he agreed and came to England for the recording. I had gotten one of the lyrics wrong on "Oh Pretty Woman" and he picked up on it straight away. He jumped up and said, "Stop the tape!"

He corrected me, then kept repeating it every half hour and looking over his glasses at me like a headmaster. We spent several days in the studio, and I learned nothing watching him play because he was magical and so idiosyncratic. It was an incredibly great experience for me.

Albert Collins was great, a sweet, lovely gentleman who was fun and easy to be around. He just blew me away. We toured together for several months and played several songs together each night, which was a treat because he was such a great, funky player. He was very intrigued by distortion, so I gave him one of my Tube Screamers. He put it on top of his amp and left it on all the time for the rest of his career.

B.B. is another legend, of course, and the first of these guys I heard as a kid. He was so relaxed and self-deprecating, a very humble guy who was lovely to be around. He came to the studio, sat down in the control room and just played.

 How did you come to own Peter Green's '59 Les Paul, and do you still have it? —*R. CARVER*

Peter discovered my group Skid Row in Dublin in the late Sixties when I was 16. He was in Fleetwood Mac at the time. Shortly after we met, the group started opening for Fleetwood Mac and I began hanging out with him—and he was one of my favorite players! At some point, he told me he was leaving the band. He was going through a head trip and wanted to get rid of his possessions. I was playing at the Marquee club and Peter asked if I wanted to borrow his '59 Les Paul, which was *the* guitar for me. I wanted it more than anything. The next day I went to his parents' house and picked it up. A few days later, he called and asked if I wanted to buy it. I said, "I can't afford it," but he said, "Sell your guitar and just give me what you get for it." I sold my SG for about 150 pounds, and he didn't take even that. He said, "I'll just take what I paid for it," which was about 120 pounds. I knew he wasn't in the best frame of mind, so I told him that if he ever wanted it back, he only had to ask for it. He said, "I will never ask for it back. I just want it to have a good home." I've had it ever since.

Why don't you ever tour the U.S.? —*KEVIN KERR*

Because I hate your president. [*laughs*] Honestly, the only time I've had real success in the U.S. was when I released *Still Got the Blues*, and even then, I didn't play many shows because it's just so expensive to get out and perform. I'm afraid it's just not viable for me. I have toured in the U.S. a few times, and I love the audiences, which are very passionate and bring out my best playing. Also, all the music I love comes from the U.S., and I find that very inspiring.

Q: **Vivian Campbell once summed up his admiration for your playing by saying you always seemed to put some "impossible" passage in your solos. Was this a conscious effort on your part?** —*ANONYMOUS*

No. If it was impossible, I couldn't have played it. Actually, I *can't* play some of my own parts. [*laughs*] My solo on "Out in the Fields," for instance, is so hard to play that I started wishing I hadn't come up with the idea. I had to do it over and over again in the studio, and I have never pulled off the run at the very end quite right live. But I didn't write it that way in order to make it difficult. I thought it was exciting, and I used to like to pack as much into a solo as possible. I was very inspired by people like George Harrison, who had 8 or 12 bars to make a statement, and I tried to approach each solo in a similar compositional sense, where I wrote it out and it was almost like a song within a song. However, my blues solos are strictly improvised.

Q: **The first time I heard "End of the World," I literally stopped my car in the middle of the road so I could hear it clearly and find out who it was. Have you ever had a similar experience?** —*JOHN KIRKPATRICK*

A few times, yes. When I was 14, I was staying in my grandmother's little wooden house in Northern Ireland, and I had a tiny transistor radio. Suddenly, an Albert King song came roaring out of it, and I was like, "Fuck, what is this?" And perhaps the best example was Eric Clapton's playing on John Mayall's "All Your Love." It was the first time a guitar had ever sounded like that—so big, passionate and intense. My friend had the Bluesbreakers album. He put it on his little stereo and it gave me the shits. My insides turned over, and that was it for me. The world was never the same place again.

STEVE
VAI

What was it like to take lessons from Joe Satriani, and could you share with us the single most important thing he taught you? —*BILL TEITGE*

My guitar lessons were everything to me when I was younger. I took them more seriously than anything else in my life. They were my conduits to freedom and helped me to discover myself. The biggest thing I learned from Joe was that whenever you approach anything on the instrument, make it musical. Make it sound and feel like a piece of music. He was always tremendously musical when he touched the instrument, and that had a big impact on me.

 Why did you decide to cut the "handle" into your Ibanez back in the day? —*DALE FLORSHEIM*

When I was playing guitar for David Lee Roth, we were preparing for a video and I was thinking about different entertaining and acrobatic things to do with the guitar. I thought, How can I swing this guitar around? I considered all the possibilities and finally realized you can't really whip the guitar around by just holding the horn or the neck. I thought, Well why don't I do something bizarre, and cut a handle in it? And it worked. Originally, it was a practical application, but eventually it became such an identifying feature of the instrument that I just kept it.

 Which is more important: great technique or raw emotion? And why? —*J.A.K. KUPETZ*

For me, I like to have both in extreme degrees. Why restrict yourself to one choice? If all you have is raw emotion but no technique, how can you express that emotion eloquently? You can be visceral with the instrument, but you'll get your point across better if you have the technique. Conversely, if you're all technique and no emotion, that'll have its particular effect, too. It's something I've battled my whole life, 'cause the textbook definition of Steve Vai is for the most part heavily weighted on the technical side of things. But I can't let that slow me down. All in all, I think a good balance of the two will get you the results you want.

 Please tell us your thoughts on the late Frank Zappa and how he influenced your playing. —*SHAYNE NYLUND*

Frank was a historic musician, and I believe his music will continue to change the quality of people's lives as they discover it. His catalog is so diverse, vast and exquisite. Frank

171

danced that fine line between being accessible and unclassifiable. A lot of contemporary pop music is wallpaper, designed to give us a little stimulation or make us feel sexy or fuel our dreams of being stars or whatever. But the world brings forth true brilliant artists, like Frank, and these people have no choice but to create. Their contributions cut right to the root of our emotional being because they're so vital to us.

On a personal level, I've transcribed many hours of Frank's guitar playing. I've stood three feet from him onstage through eight months of touring and watched him play at least an hour and a half of soloing per night. What I discovered was that I would never really have a handle on his guitar playing. Frank was always being creative with the instrument. Although he had a particular technique, he would take that technique into different areas, and that was the crux of his brilliance. I learned from him that, although we're all kind of limited to a degree by our individual techniques, we can instill our techniques into different fields and get something weird and different.

 How did you make ends meet before you became Steve Vai the Guitar Hero? Were you ever Steve Vai the Fast-Food Guy? —WOOLLEY

Some people *still* consider me Steve Vai the Fast-Food Guy. [*laughs*] I think the attitude that we have toward our job can really reflect the way we go about making our music. I never expected to become famous or successful, but it didn't matter, 'cause I knew as long as I got to play the instrument I would be happy. When I was younger I had to wash dishes; I drove an ice-cream truck; I cut lawns. But here's how I looked at it: these jobs helped me to have time to make the music I liked, and they afforded me the funds to buy a guitar. You can have a positive attitude toward the menial jobs you may have to take if you can realize that they're enabling you to play your instrument. They're a means to an end, not an end unto themselves.

 What is the meaning of your symbol with the pyramid, triangle and eye? —NICK HAWKINS

When I drew that up I was studying a lot of metaphysics. Historically, the pyramid is shrouded in mystique, and the eye in the middle was inspired by the all-seeing "spiritual" or "third" eye, which gives you the power of inner sight. But the truth is, I don't follow any of that stuff anymore. My spiritual goals are much higher now, and I think that stuff can be a deterrent in the path to further spiritual development. Although I built those symbols and have used them in the past, they're all really meaningless.

Do you ever listen to your early material and say to yourself, "What the hell was I thinking?"

—BRANDON BRAY

All the time. I actually like my music a lot and listen to it quite often. It's funny when I look back at things I've created or written because, for creative people, everything they do becomes a snapshot of their psyche at that particular time. So when I listen to something I did a while ago, I'm kind of reliving those moments, and to a certain extent, I'm revisiting the person I was back then. Through that process, I'm able to see my growth as well as my deficiencies. There are definitely pieces I listen to that make me think, Wow what a weird guy. It's an educational process, but mostly it's just quite enjoyable.

The important aspects of spirituality don't reside in rituals or ceremonies or numbers or pyramids.

 What equipment were you using for the guitar duel in the movie *Crossroads*? And was it difficult to get beaten by that guy [*Ralph Macchio*] from *The Karate Kid*? —*BRANDON LITTLE*

I used my "Green Meanie" Charvel through a Carvin X100B amp with a Roland SDE-3000 delay and an MXR distortion pedal. Was it hard to get beat? Ladies and gentlemen, Ralph Macchio is a wonderful actor—but he did not play one single note of the guitar in the film! All the slide guitar playing you hear is Ry Cooder. All the picked guitar you hear is me. It's shocking that people think he actually beat me. It's the movies. It's all fake!

What *was* difficult was that I had to create something that I beat myself at. The first time I did it, we filmed 12 days for 16 hours a day. And when they went back to the edit bay and cut the movie together, they realized I didn't lose bad enough. So they called me back a month later and I had to go in and screw up more.

 If you had to design a Mount Rushmore for guitar players, what four faces would you put there? —*ABEL SANCHEZ*

I'm a rock guitarist, so I'll speak in those terms. If I had to point out guitar players who reshaped the instrument I would pick Jimi Hendrix, Jimmy Page, Edward Van Halen and Stevie Ray Vaughan. In their fields, these people really had an impact on the way we think about rock guitar.

 Do you find that there are still things you can improve on, guitarwise? Or have you mastered the instrument? —*KOSTAS MPOURNAS*

I'm so far from mastering the instrument. Every time I pick up the instrument, I find something I can improve upon. One specific thing I'm trying to develop is visualization. If you don't have a vision of where you're going, you're really just running in circles. So when I think about where I want to go as a guitar player, I visualize myself as a person standing onstage and creating a voice that speaks clearly to people. I picture my body language, my face and everything that I'm doing as being completely in balance and one with each other. If I imagine it, I'll become it.

LENNY
KRAVITZ

Q: **What musical instrument in your collection has the most meaning to you and why?** —*GUITAR KEVIN*

The 1959 Les Paul "Goldtop" that I have used on every record. It's been sanded down to this sort of nasty, very dull green color, like root beer mixed with gold. It's got the most beautiful PAFs I've ever heard in it. That's my number-one studio ax. In fact, it doesn't leave the studio. I got it years ago, probably on my second tour ever. There was this poor gentleman that came to the backstage door, and said that he had a bunch of instruments that he wanted to sell. He said, "Look, I have to fight this [*lawsuit*]. I don't want to go to jail. I have to sell my gear." So he brought out this group of guitars, including that Les Paul. He also had the Gibson Skylark amp that was used on "Are You Gonna Go My Way." I ended up buying the whole lot, but I felt bad for him that he had to part with those instruments.

Q: **You've never been shy about being a Kiss fan. Your song "Dig In" reminds me a lot of Kiss. Was it intentional or maybe a case of influences subconsciously finding their way into your music?** —*JIM HAGERMAN*

It's never intentional. But every now and again I'll do a song and say, "Oh, I've got a bit of this thing, and a bit of that." Besides putting on the most amazing show and having this genius vision of characters that will last forever, Kiss wrote some great rock and roll songs that have incredible hooks—especially the original lineup. Their first several records were very raunchy and raw, and Ace Frehley is a really underrated guitar player. So from listening to them as a kid, I absorbed some of their sensibility of writing rock songs that have a pop appeal and big hooks.

Q: **I read an interview in the late Eighties where you ragged on all the then-modern equipment, particularly Kramer and Charvel. Is there any new gear that has gotten you to soften your stance, or do you still choose vintage or nothing at all?** —*LORNE CARTER*

I don't know if I was ragging on them. I was just saying that I prefer other guitars. In fact, one of my first guitars was a Charvel. I had a fuchsia-colored Charvel with a pearl overcoat and one pickup that I used on a lot of sessions and gigs. I do prefer Gibsons and Fenders, but I think those other guitars—in the hands of the right people playing the right music—are amazing. Obviously I'm a huge Eddie Van Halen fan. I just got into really classic gear. And for my music, it has the right sound.

I am 15 years old and play lead guitar in a band. We play every weekend, and I am eventually hoping to go on tour and get signed. If you could go back in time and give yourself one piece of advice before you entered a career in music, what would that be?

—BRAD

First thing, I would've learned more about the business. I did read books, and I did try to learn as much as I could. But you can never know enough about how the business works as far as when you sign, what you're giving up and what you're getting. It's your music and your property, and you have to be very careful with it. The one thing I did right was that I was always myself. Remain yourself at all times. Don't go in a direction just because the company says it's a trend and you'll have a bigger hit because of it. As far as I'm concerned, if you're just chasing what's hip at the moment, you won't last.

Q: **When did you first pick up a guitar, and what were the first songs that you practiced?** —*DUSTIN NELSON*

I first started playing guitar when I was about eight years old. The first song I learned was, of course, "Smoke on the Water," which at that time was everybody's first song. That and a song by John Denver called "Country Roads." I went to summer camp and learned that song by the campfire.

Q: **You're a fan of lots of musical styles, but I've never heard you reference heavy metal. Do you like any of those bands? If so, who?** —*MIKE CONCH*

My rock age really started in L.A., because growing up in New York I was primarily into soul, R&B and jazz. So when I got to L.A., I started with Led Zeppelin. Then I became a Kiss fan, which is something that a lot of kids at that time wouldn't admit, as if it wasn't cool. Then I got into AC/DC and, later, Metallica. So those are the main ones. I never got so much into speed metal.

Q: **In 1991 you recorded a song with Slash, "Always on the Run." Recently, he put out a record featuring a lot of great guest players. Would you consider doing an album like that? If so, who would you want to work with?** —*LUKE*

Well, I can honestly say that I've already gotten to work with so many of my heroes. I've worked with Bob Dylan, Tom Petty, Mick Jagger, Michael Jackson, Curtis Mayfield, Bootsy Collins, Prince, Aretha Franklin... I guess most of the other people I'd like to work with aren't here anymore.

Q: **You wrote the song "Rock and Roll Is Dead" years ago. What do you think of the current state of guitar-driven rock? Are things in need of a revival, or is all hope lost?** —*MIKE HOLMES*

When I wrote that song, I wasn't so much saying that rock and roll was dead; I was writing the song directly to these bands I knew who thought they had to live a certain way in order to be so-called "rock and rollers." They had to have the drugs and the cliché lifestyle. And I was saying that's a dead idea. You don't have to be a drug addict and abuse yourself. You can be anybody you want to be and still be rock and roll.

DEAR GUITAR HERO

MICHAEL
SCHENKER

Q: **How old were you when you started playing guitar, and what inspired you to start playing?** —*KEITH LOEB*

I was around nine years old, but I had been very keen on music since I was three or four. I always loved going around the house singing and expressing my love for rhythm by banging on pots and pans and stuff like that. My dad played violin and my mom played piano, so I would fool around on those, and on my brother Rudolf's 16th birthday, he got a guitar. When he would go to work, I would play his guitar—even though it was against his wishes.

Q: **Who were some of your early guitar heroes?** —*MIKE BENTIVOGLIO*

When I started playing, I hadn't heard about guys like Jimmy Page and Jeff Beck, so for me it was more about bands like the Shadows [*the British guitar group*]—instrumental music, clean guitar sounds and so on. I knew from listening to that type of music that the guitar was something I wanted to pursue. I didn't hear my first distorted guitar until I was around 13 or 14, which was when bands like Led Zeppelin started getting popular. During those years all I did was copy anything I heard that had that distorted guitar sound.

Q: **What was the first guitar you ever owned?** —*RITA DULLAGHAN*

I played whatever my brother didn't need anymore—it's the same way that I got my suits and clothes. [*laughs*] Whatever he had first, I had second. And that lasted for a while, but eventually I realized that I had my own idea of what I wanted. In the beginning we had a Framus and a Hofner, and then my brother went to a big-bodied Gibson and I went more for the Fenders, like the Jazzmaster. Then I got a Les Paul Custom, a Les Paul Deluxe, and I ended up with the V.

Q: **Do you still suffer from stage fright?** —*JOHN LUFTIG*

It doesn't exist for me anymore. I don't know exactly what made it go away, but it did. It's not something that happened overnight, but in the past few years it has slowly gone away.

Q: **How did you come to join the Scorpions?** —*JOHN ZANE*

My brother always got me my gigs in the early days. I had been in bands since I was 11, and one day my brother told me that he wanted me to hook up with this great

DEAR GUITAR HERO

SCOTT
IAN

OF ANTHRAX

Q: You always have such a great, crunchy tone. What is the key element to your sound, and what is your setup? —*ROBERT STONE*

I think the key element is my right hand; specifically, the way I pick. I lean in really heavy. If you're playing rhythm, especially in the kind of music Anthrax plays, you can't pussyfoot around; you've *gotta* dig in to get that edge. I can play through any setup with some kind of gain and master volume, and it will sound like me because of my right hand. That's the trick to getting the crunch. As far as my setup goes, I'm currently using a Randall V2, which is the second generation of the Vmax head. I have a prototype, and it sounds incredible.

Q: In the early days of Anthrax, you guys had much better and crisper production than any of your contemporaries. Was that a conscious decision or a happy accident? How did you achieve that? —*SCOTTY BROWN*

Did we? [*laughs*] I don't know, I thought Metallica's records sounded pretty damn good. Our attitude about making records has always been to capture how we sound live in the studio, and to make it sound good and clear. But it's no happy accident—it's what we do.

We were always working to achieve the vision we had in our heads of how the record should ultimately sound. Most of our studio time is spent getting the right tones. Once we start recording, we move pretty fast; it's making sure everything sounds right that takes time.

Q: Anthrax are one of the best riffing metal bands. When it comes to song-writing, does one person write the riffs and does the group help turn them into songs? —*FRANKIE TALOTTA*

Our songwriting process has evolved over the years. I started Anthrax with [*bassist*] Danny Lilker, and together we wrote the first album, *Fistful of Metal* [1984], in the years leading up to when we recorded it. Once [*drummer*] Charlie [*Benante*] joined the band for *Spreading the Disease* [1985], he became part of the songwriting process, too, 'cause he was also a guitarist.

By the time *Among the Living* [1987] rolled around, Charlie was writing just as many riffs as I was. It evolved to where I wrote all the lyrics and Charlie was the main riff writer, which took a huge weight off of my back. It wasn't until recently that I had more musical input. *We've Come for You All* [2003] was the first album in ages that I wrote riffs for. From *Among the Living* to our last record, 80 to 90 percent of the riffs were written by Charlie.

Q: **How did Anthrax come up with the idea to collaborate with Public Enemy?** [*Anthrax and Public Enemy toured together in 1991 and re-recorded PE's 1988 hit "Bring the Noise."*] **Did you have any sense that it was going to be so groundbreaking?** —*JOHN ELSTER*

I never thought it was going to be groundbreaking. They were my favorite band at the time and I was just looking for a way to work with them, 'cause I loved them so much. Anthrax had already recorded "I'm the Man," [*the 1987 hit single on which they merged heavy metal and rap*], so we kinda opened the door ourselves with that song.

The collaboration started out as a simple idea when we were tracking *Persistence of Time* [*1990*]. I had been listening to "Bring the Noise" and wrote a cool-sounding riff for it. On the last day of recording basic tracks with Charlie, I said, "Hey, I've got this idea to cover 'Bring the Noise.' Let's work out the arrangement." We spent, like, 20 minutes doing that, and then we tracked it. It sounded so killer, we decided to send it to Chuck [*D, Public Enemy lead rapper*] and asked him to do "Bring the Noise" over it.

Q: **I read that when you downpick, your thumb hits the string. What does this technique add to your sound?** —*RICHARD EVANS*

It does? [*laughs*] I guess my thumb does rub the string, 'cause the left side of my picking thumb is supercalloused and the nail always gets fucked up. But I have no idea what it does for the sound. A lot of my index fingernail hits the string, too. Without fail, that nail splits about three shows into each tour. It's actually splitting right now, and it hurts! [*laughs*] All this happens 'cause I dig in and try to push the notes out as hard as possible.

Q: **I've always thought Anthrax had more of a hardcore influence than bands like Metallica and Megadeth. Do you agree? If so, do you think it's a result of being from New York City?** —*RICHIE U.*

Yeah, I would agree. We were certainly more into hardcore than Metallica and Megadeth. From early on, even before *Fistful of Metal*, we were listening to a lot of English hardcore, like Discharge, G.B.H. and the Exploited. Then we got into bands from the New York scene, like Agnostic Front and the Cro-Mags, and from there we got into Bad Brains, D.R.I., Corrosion of Conformity and Suicidal Tendencies. Metallica certainly listened to hardcore—they covered Discharge on *Garage, Inc.*—but I don't think the influence was expressed in their music as strongly as it was in ours.

187

MIKE NESS

Q: In the early days, you were using an SG. What made you switch over to Les Pauls with P90s? Also, what string gauge are you currently playing with? —*RICKY BREEZ*

I switched over to Les Pauls in the late Eighties when I realized they weren't as heavy as I thought. And I really liked the sustain that they have. Eventually, I toured with Neil Young and realized that I liked the Deluxes because of the slightly tapered neck. I picked the brain of Neil Young's guitar tech that tour. I watched his tech pull the thin mini-humbucker out of a Les Paul Deluxe, drop it in the trash can, and put a P90 in it. I've been using P90s ever since. As far as strings go, we use Ernie Ball. I believe it's the 10–52 set. It's got heavier strings at the bottom, where you need it, but you still have the flexibility in the upper strings.

Q: The production on [2004's] *Sex, Love and Rock 'n' Roll* is noticeably bigger than on previous Social Distortion albums, especially the guitar sound. What setup did you use to get that massive tone? —*COHEN HEART*

I'm pretty sure it was my Fender Bassman. That's the motor that drives this machine. But I can tell you that, as good as those songs might have been, we've left them in the dust with this new record. The problem with that record was that things got a little over-compressed. We were still in the mindset of stacking guitars and all that. I've learned now that less is better. We've got the tones already, so it's just about getting the instruments to tape the right way. I mean, you listen to an old Bad Company record and you hear four instruments playing. That's it. But it's recorded fat, through analog equipment and a nice board, and captured with proper miking techniques. So we're going back to the basics.

Q: Your music has gotten me through some of the roughest parts of my life, specifically when I was getting over my drinking problems. Did you ever think that by sorting out your problems and then writing about them you'd be doing a service to other people? —*TONY*

People tell me all the time, "Your music's gotten me through tough times." And I just tell them, "Me too!" You think you're just writing songs, just playing music, but you don't realize that music really can be a very spiritual and emotional thing. That's what it always was for me, but I never expected that I could do the same thing for others.

The new record's called *Hard Times and Nursery Rhymes*. At first, I thought it was just a humorous metaphor for a bunch of guys in a band who are all kind of immature. We have a hard time functioning in the real world, but out on the road, we're able to perfect our craft—or, at least, we're in the *pursuit* of perfecting it. When we're onstage, it's the one element of our lives that we have control over. But when I started to think about it more, I thought how nursery rhymes are something you read to a child to calm them down or to help them through a hard time. And, really, to me, that's all music is.

 Q: **You're into custom car and bike culture. What are you riding or building these days?** —*CRAIG WILLIAMSON*

Man, I've always got a project going. I just finished a 1937 Chevy pickup lowrider and just put a new motor in the '50 Merc. We've got it lowered now, but it's too nice to chop. My goal is to get the '37 chopped this year, probably by Cole Foster of Salinas Boys Customs.

 Q: **Does Billy Zoom modify your Bassman heads, and does that mod include putting a tube rectifier in each one?** —*MIKE KRUG*

Billy Zoom modified a couple amps for me back in the early days, but the last 10 years I've been using Fred Taccone from Divided by 13, who does a similar mod. I'm not sure what it entails technically, but it allows me to get a good tone at a lower volume. Instead of going to 10, I only have to go to about 6. I have it going through eight Marshall speakers, which just spreads it nicely, like butter.

 Q: **Your live sound is amazing! What cabs and effects do you use with your Fender Bassman?** —*PHILIPP GUÉTAT*

I use two 1960 Marshall reissue cabs with Greenback speakers. I haven't had to replace those speakers in a long time. I have one Boss stomp box for a slight volume and gain boost for solos. In the studio, I might use a little delay from time to time, but not too much.

 Q: **Since the unfortunate passing of [*founding guitarist*] Dennis Danell, how have the guitar playing dynamics changed in the band with the addition of Jonny Wickersham?** —*MIKE HEBERT*

Dennis was a dear friend of mine. He and I started this band. He wasn't in the band because he was a hot guitar player—he and I were partners in crime, and best friends. I taught Dennis how to play guitar, and, you know, I could only teach him so much. But when we began playing together, I saw what an infinite amount you could do with two guitars. When Jonny joined, I knew that he was going to be bringing a lot to the band because of his abilities. And he's great. What I love most is that he gives me textures that embellish the songs.

Q: **Your solos just flow so easily with the songs. They're almost like vocal lines. What advice do you have when it comes to how to write a good solo? I seem to be getting stuck in the pentatonic box.** —*JAMIE SWEETEN*
Well, that is something I do subconsciously with my leads: make them a continuation of the vocal line, or a variation on it. You need to bring a hook or something from the melody into the solo. Otherwise, it can sound like a studio session player, where there's a solo that has nothing to do with the song. You really have to get into the song, listen to the melody and figure out how to wrap your solo in and around that thing. But I get stuck, too.

When I was 17 or 18, I had an accident where I almost cut my index finger completely off. I can only bend it about halfway. Since Jonny joined the band, I've relinquished a lot to him. There's a lot of stuff I have Jonny do, because I can't do it. A lot of people don't know that, but I'm kind of handicapped. I do an A minor starting with my middle finger. But I take pride in my rhythm guitar. I think people underestimate that sometimes. Listen to AC/DC, and you'll see why it's important. That rhythm guitar is driving the band.

MIKAEL ÅKERFELDT & FREDRIK ÅKESSON

OF OPETH

Q: Mikael, when Opeth released their first album, *Orchid*, in 1994, you guys were associated with black metal. At that point, where did you see yourself fitting within the Scandinavian black/death metal scene? —*PETE SANDUSKY*

ÅKERFELDT Even though we were part of the black metal scene, I didn't feel like we really belonged to it; we were more like hippies. I loved black metal and still do, but I think we were trying to do a sort of metal-hippie-minstrel thing. For some reason we were accepted among the "Norwegian mafia," as we called the bands that were in and out of jail. Now I'm friends with many of those guys.

Q: Mikael, when you began writing *Watershed*, did you have any specific objectives in mind, like a concept you wanted to explore? —*JOE TRITTLE*

ÅKERFELDT The lyrics on *Watershed* are conceptual, in a way, but I didn't have any idea of what I wanted when I started. In general, the process is usually just a matter of crossing my fingers and hoping I'll come up with something cool. [*laughs*] And so far I've been lucky.

Q: Fredrik, how does playing with Opeth compare to your experience performing in Arch Enemy? Did you have to dramatically change your style when you joined Opeth? —*VINCENT CULLEN*

ÅKESSON There are many differences between the two bands. Arch Enemy was a great time for me; I had a blast. With Opeth, I feel more involved in the band—although I did discover when I joined Opeth that I needed to work on my acoustic playing and my fingerpicking techniques.

Q: What kind of players did you guys look up to when you first started playing guitar? —*CHRISTIAN EBBS*

ÅKERFELDT For me it was Dave Murray and Adrian Smith, Yngwie Malmsteen, Matthias Jabs from the Scorpions, K.K. Downing, Glenn Tipton, Ritchie Blackmore... As you can see, I was into the metal players. When you're a young guitar player, I guess it's kind of inevitable that you end up liking the guys who play really fast. [*laughs*]

ÅKESSON I also liked Ritchie Blackmore, as well as Ace Frehley and Angus Young, when I was starting out. But what literally got me to start practicing more was when I first saw Michael Schenker. After that I started getting into Yngwie, Uli Jon Roth, Cacaphony with Jason Becker and Marty Friedman, and Racer X with Paul Gilbert.

Åkerfeldt (*left*) and Åkesson

 What guitars are you playing, and what do you like about them?
—BRYAN MICHAELS

ÅKERFELDT I play a custom-made PRS 24. I don't know why I need the extra two frets, but I'm sure it makes it more expensive! [*laughs*] I've spent a lifetime trying to find a guitar that has everything. I grew up loving the Stratocaster, but it just couldn't get the fat tone I needed. I think the PRS is almost like a combination between a Strat and a Les

Paul. PRS makes really reliable guitars. Not only do they sound great but you can throw them into the wall, like I do, and they won't break. [*laughs*]

ÅKESSON With Opeth I use a PRS Singlecut 250 with a Mark Tremonti pickup, and I also use ESP Eclipses.

Q: **What were the circumstances surrounding guitarist Peter Lindgren leaving the band?** —*CONNOR FINCH*

ÅKERFELDT Peter had been in the band for a long time, and I think anyone who's in a touring band and works as much as we do will tell you it's a difficult situation. I have two kids and a wife back home, and it's hard to be away. Peter has a masters degree, and when we got off tour, he started to see what he could do with it. Also, I've written most of the albums on my own, and I think he must have felt a little left out. His interest in the band and touring just seemed to fade away. I guess it got to the point where he couldn't give 100 percent, so he left. While I now see that it's for the better, it's always going to trouble me, I guess. It's the same with the departure of Martin Lopez [*former Opeth drummer who was replaced by Martin Axenrot in 2006*].

Q: **When writing such long songs, what do you keep in mind to make sure they stay interesting?** —*WILLIAM WILLIAMSON*

ÅKERFELDT It's hard for me to say. I like the droning type of riffs that last forever, but I also like when things are going on all of the time and you have no idea what's happening. It's actually difficult not to write long songs when I want to incorporate all the acoustic parts, interludes, clean vocal bits and that kind of stuff. It's just my style. But it's hard for me to say what keeps a long song interesting, because I guess it's really in the ear of the beholder.

Q: **What do you do when you're low on inspiration?** —*OSCAR ALBUQUERQUE*

ÅKERFELDT I just keep playing through it. I usually know when I don't have any inspiration because I start playing shitty blues licks and horrible solos. [*laughs*] So I'll take a break, have a cup of coffee, check emails, look at some porn [*laughs*], and then I go back to the guitar. If you can't come up with great stuff, a little break can usually help.

DEAR GUITAR HERO

NEAL
SCHON

OF JOURNEY

How do you feel that "Don't Stop Believing" was used in the series finale of The Sopranos?" —*TOBY DEAN WALCOTT*

I didn't know it was in the final episode until after it aired. I'm not on the computer every day, and the guy that works our publishing sends us emails, and I guess I just missed it. But I certainly found out when my phone started ringing off the hook! [*laughs*] When I finally watched the episode, I thought it was very cool. Once again, that song prevails with flying stripes. The ball teams have all been using it, and now these guys.

 I heard you found your singer, Arnel Pineda, on YouTube. —*CARL THOMAS*

That's exactly what happened. When Steve Perry stepped down, I set out to look for a new singer. Obviously, we were looking for a tenor voice, but I wasn't looking for a Steve Perry clone. I needed the right tenor who could take us into the future and still do a good job with our older catalog. I wasn't looking forward to doing auditions and flying in people from everywhere. So I thought YouTube would be a good alternative, because most all the performances posted there are live. And I figured if the guy sounds good live, then he's got it.

But after a couple days of searching I'd almost given up hope. It was really depressing. Then all of a sudden I saw this clip from a guy, Arnel Pineda, covering a Survivor song and he sounded amazing. So I tracked him down in Manila, Philippines. Then I had to convince him it was really me and not a hoax! [*laughs*]

 You are one of the few guitarists who use their pinkie with such dexterity. Did you make a conscious effort to develop pinkie strength to use it for solos? —*DAVID BERNSTEIN*

Everything I do in solos is based on something that's come to me naturally. It's nothing I've really worked on. But I've been playing for so many years that I think I've naturally expanded in different directions over time. I don't practice, but I have strengthened my fingers just by playing new patterns and scales throughout the years.

Do you ever think about where your musical career would have gone if you accepted Eric Clapton's offer to join Derek and the Dominos? —*MORRISON DAY*

You know, I've actually thought about that a lot. Part of me kicks myself in the butt for

I think many of your memorable solos come from *Escape* [*Journey's 1981 album*]. Do you feel that that album epitomized the high point of your playing style at that time?
—SHANNON ALDRIDGE

Yeah, that album was one of the heights of our career. There were really no boundaries at that time. We were trying a lot of stuff and mixing a lot of different types of music together. Actually, that was one of the reasons that a lot of critics used to pan us, because they couldn't categorize us.

not doing it, because I was such a fan of Eric Clapton. But he wanted me to move to England. I had just turned 15 and wasn't quite ready to leave the Bay Area. Also, I had a gut instinct about it. After all, the whole band was, let's just say, well medicated. [*laughs*] I remember walking backstage, like, 10 minutes before they went on, and everybody was snoozing. [*laughs*] So I was like, I don't think this thing is gonna last that long. I would have loved to do it, but I think I made the right choice by going with Santana.

 You have played with so many great musicians. Are there any other artists you'd love to work with? —*NIKKI "BELLA" DONNA*

I've been working on a project at the Record Plant in Sausalito, and everyone is on this thing: Stevie Wonder, Carlos Santana, Buddy Miles, Randy Jackson... But when I think, Who do I really *have* to play with, no one person comes to mind. That said, I'm open-minded about playing with anyone that approaches me...if they're good. [*laughs*]

 What do you recommend to a player who is seeking to be as fluent as possible in many rock styles? —*PATRICK MCMANN*

I think it all comes down to what you listen to. It's said that you are what you eat, and to that I would add, you are what you listen to. I think you can't be close-minded when it comes to listening. I listen to everything from classical music to John McLaughlin. Compared to when I was a kid—when there were, like, 10 players I could point to as my favorites—today there are so many people for kids to listen to and learn from.

DEAR GUITAR HERO

PAUL
GILBERT

Q: When you used that drill-bit pick, how exactly did you put the pick on the drill bit? [*Gilbert used a cordless drill with three picks attached to a dowel rod to perform the last 16 measures of the solo to the Mr. Big song "Daddy, Brother, Lover, Little Boy (The Drill Song)"*] —*ROB RODRIGUES*

The first time I tried it, I attached the picks with Super Glue, but it wasn't strong enough on its own, and the picks went flying off. The materials you need are a wooden dowel rod, which you cut to whatever length fits your bit; thin guitar picks, because the thick ones don't sound as good; and lock washers, which keep the picks from rotating. First, drill a small hole through the top of each pick. Put the lock washers in between each pick, and then stick a little wood screw through the whole bunch and screw it to the top of the dowel rod. Douse it with some Krazy Glue or epoxy, let it dry, and you're all set to go.

Q: If you had to pick just one song to play for someone who has never heard your music, which one would you pick? —*ERNIE ZUPON*

"Scarified" [Second Heat, *1987, Racer X*] is a good one, but I was never completely happy with the studio performance. I got the point across, but it wasn't as clean as I would have liked. I wanted it robotically clean. "Superheroes" " [Superheroes, *2001, Racer X*] is a pretty good one, too. It's mixed better—my playing's a little clearer and not soaked in reverb, like it was on the old records. "Green-Tinted Sixties Mind" [Lean Into It, *1991*] is probably my favorite Mr. Big track, because it has things that are simultaneously melodically and technically inventive. And solo, I think the whole *Get Out of My Yard* [*2006*] instrumental CD is certainly a monument of what I have to say on the guitar. It's probably the best one of all, because it's nothing but guitar.

Q: Your alternate-picking technique never ceases to amaze me. I always feel stiff when I reach higher speeds, and I'm wondering what exercises you'd recommend to develop greater alternate-picking proficiency. —*DAN*

Judging from most of the students I've seen, I would guess that you need to work on your fretting hand. Most people have a problem coordinating both hands. In general, when I see people whose picking sounds wrong, it's not because their picking isn't fast enough but because their fretting hand isn't fast enough; they just don't realize that. I really thought I would never be able to pick fast, so I worked a lot on my fretting hand. I didn't do any significant fast picking until I'd been playing for about eight

Who do you consider to be the best shredder on the planet?

—LURINA GROSS

Well, I'm still getting used to the word "shred." When I first wanted to play guitar fast, there was no such word. I guess Eddie Van Halen was the first player I noticed playing fast. What he did was obviously cool from a musical standpoint, but it was also athletic, and athleticism is probably the distinguishing characteristic of shred. I really liked that about Eddie. Same with Yngwie: he was probably the last guy whose music I sat down with and tried to figure out. His picking technique was just so exciting. Even though you could hear Uli Jon Roth and Ritchie Blackmore in Yngwie's playing, he really cranked it up a few notches.

years. And by that time my fretting hand could perform Van Halen–style ascending sixes, like you hear on "Spanish Fly," the same kind of sixes George Lynch did in the Dokken days.

I was also inspired by the album *Universal Juveniles,* by the band Max Webster, whose guitarist is Kim Mitchell. The opening track, "In the World of Giants," starts off with some descending sixes played on the highest two strings. They're medium tempo by today's shred standards, but when I first heard the album in the Eighties, they sounded blisteringly fast. And more than that, they're played really well. The notes sound really good, and I think that is a much bigger accomplishment and a nobler goal than to play as fast as possible. You have to play well before you can play fast, at least if you want it to be listenable. The same techniques that allow you to sound good when playing slow apply to playing fast. So work on playing well before you work on playing fast.

 You play some of the coolest guitars I have ever seen. What was the inspiration behind your Ibanez "fringe" guitar and how hard is it to play a guitar with a fringed neck? —*CARLOS DENIDA*

The fringe guitar is nice to play because it keeps your hands dry. If you're onstage with lots of stage lights and it's hot, the fringe cleans all the sweat off your fingers. The idea really just came from desperation. In the old Racer X days we almost only played in Los Angeles, so the same audience would see us every gig. We knew if we did the same show with the same stuff, people would get bored. So we were always trying to think of something new we could do to keep their interest.

 I am a guitar pick enthusiast, and you are probably my favorite artist to collect. What made you decide to print prices on your picks? —*ANTHONY STROEHMAN*

I discovered that pick-collecting fans were coming to the shows just to get the picks; they weren't even staying for the shows. They would just hang out and try to catch us from the bus to the venue. I started printing prices on them when I found the picks were going for exorbitant prices on eBay. I made a set of four: $10, $25, $75, $1,000; I was curious to see if someone would pay $1,000 because that's what was on the pick. So I put them into circulation. While I don't know what ever happened, it gives me a warm feeling inside thinking about it. [*laughs*]

203

Your sense of humor sets you apart from other guitarists. What's the funniest thing that has ever happened to you while on tour?

—COREY GIES

The funniest thing I remember is getting the drill caught in my hair after I was done playing my solo with it. I was onstage doing the heavy metal put-your-hand-next-to-your-ear signal to let the audience know they should go crazy and make noise. But when I did that, the drill in my hand was still spinning, and it grabbed my curly locks and got hopelessly tangled. Luckily for me, Billy Sheehan came out and saved the day with a bass solo. That's actually one of the lesser-known uses of a bass player: to save the day when your guitarist gets a drill caught in his hair.

I'm a big fan of your guitar tone. What do you consider to be the key element to your sound? —*THOMAS HARTLEY*

I first began having success picking on a guitar that wasn't plugged in. I was picking really hard so I could hear it acoustically, and when I plugged into an amp, I was surprised that it didn't sound very good. I discovered that the way I attack the string really affects the tone. Modifying your picking attack—for clean tone, distortion and playing on an acoustic—makes a huge difference in the sound.

 Have you ever thought about doing a traditional blues album? —*PAULY*

I did a bluesy album [Raw Blues Power, *2002*] with my uncle, Jimi Kidd, who was a huge influence on me when I was younger. But traditional blues? I don't know. I like some of the really dirty traditional blues, like John Lee Hooker. But for that stuff, those guys are out of tune and the bars go too long, and you hear the bass player change a second later than the other guys. That stuff really gives it its down-and-dirty feeling. I think I'd have to start drinking a lot more to really do it right. [*laughs*] I don't know if it's possible. When you say "traditional" I take it seriously enough to know probably not to go there!

DEAR GUITAR HERO

GEORGE
LYNCH

Q: I've always been fascinated by the Skeleton Guitar you used in the "It's Not Love" video. I'm pretty sure it's an ESP. Could you give some history and possibly some facts about this guitar? —*JACK CALDIERO*

Absolutely. My friend J. Frog and I worked on that guitar for about a year. He does prosthetic monster makeup for horror movies. He had the gist of the idea, and I helped him musically fine-tune it. We carved this thing out of one solid piece of wood. It was an incredible amount of work. The original has an actual gold tooth that J. pulled out of his mouth and stuck on there. That guitar looked amazing, but it was very unplayable and didn't sound very good. I played it in Dokken for a while, and it ended up going to the Hard Rock Café in Hollywood. Then ESP ended up building 25 of them, which were much better-sounding and -playing guitars. I still have one of those, which I use.

Q: What advice would you give to an intermediate guitarist who wants to increase the speed and accuracy of his fret hand? I feel that my picking ability far outshines my fret-hand skills. —*JOHN DANEK*

That's interesting, because you usually hear of the opposite happening. One exercise that I used to do is work my fretting hand without using my pinkie and ring finger. Try that, and also work on hammer-ons and pull-offs. In fact, I'd suggest trying to take the right hand out of the mix completely. It's like Hendrix back in the day—his picking arm would be in the air, but he'd *still* be ripping it up with his fret hand.

Q: I know you were into bodybuilding pretty seriously. How did you keep your fingers so limber for pulling off your jaw dropping licks? I find that the more I get involved with lifting the worse my playing becomes because my hands become so tight. —*DAVE HALLWAY*

That's absolutely true, and I experienced that when I was into heavy lifting for a little while back in the mid Nineties to 2000. I was out with Dokken and I cared more about bodybuilding than playing guitar. I found that any time I had an extended solo, I would get static contractions in my forearm. Any solo longer than 30 seconds would make my hand turn into "the claw." It was silliness, so I backed way off the exercise, and my playing has gotten tremendously better and more relaxed. It's okay to stay in shape, of course, but up to a point. I used to make fun of all those guys who looked like body-builders onstage, and then I became one. [*laughs*] I don't know how that happened. All of sudden I was looking like Rambo. All I needed was a flame-throwing guitar.

What do you consider to be the most important thing to achieving your sound? —*NASIR HABIB*

Well, I rely a lot on delay. My favorite tool for that is an old Echoplex, even though there are so many digital delays out there that are easier to use. I rely on it for solos, of course, but I also like a little bit of slap on my rhythm playing. I like how it gives you a rhythm to play off of, and if you're playing kinda bouncy it gives you some depth.

Additionally, I've learned a lot in the last decade about tone. I've gotten around to the idea that less is more. In a less-powerful pickup, like the Screamin' Demon and the Seymour Duncan Super V, the magnets are not as strong as some of the older stuff I used to use. I mean, I used to use the *strongest* pickup I could find. I used to use a metal pick, and sometimes the pickup pole pieces were so magnetic that they would grab the pick out of my finger. [*laughs*] I've learned to play with a little less distortion so that the dynamics really come out in my playing.

I would like to ask you about the Japanese letters on your ESP Kamikaze guitar. Is it true that your ex-wife asked for these letters to be printed on the guitar so that groupies wouldn't get close to you? —*JOHN PANAGOPOULOS*

I've never been able to figure out exactly what it says. I've been over to Asia and people have told me it says everything from "I'm George Lynch and I have many children" to "I don't take very many showers" to "kamikaze." But I can't read those characters, so who really knows.

I heard you took over Randy Rhoads' guitar lessons at Musonia School of Music after he left to play with Ozzy Osbourne. Is that true, and what was your relationship with Randy? —*CODY SAUNDERS*

It is true. I had been up for the Ozzy gig on three different occasions, one being the time Randy got it. Sometime after the audition, I was doing a show at the Starwood, and Randy showed up with his mom, Delores. He came up to me and let me know how the decision went. He said, "I've got some good news and some bad news. The bad news is that you didn't get the Ozzy gig and I did. The good news is that you get to teach guitar at my mom's school because I won't be able to...for $5 dollars an hour." [*laughs*] Funny thing about it was that Randy was kind of a good-looking guy, so he had all these female students that weren't even interested in playing guitar. Then when I came in there, half of them quit immediately. [*laughs*] It was pretty brutal. I guess I didn't have the bow tie or something. [*laughs*]

I've read that while on tour, you would have the tubes in your amplifier changed out before every show. Is this true, and if so what was the benefit of doing so? —*JAY ROSZATYCKI*

Well, I used to do that when I was in Dokken, and there is absolutely no benefit to it. All I can say is that you find yourself doing ridiculous things when you're making lots of money and playing in front of thousands of people every night. You need someone to polish your guitar picks and hold your umbrella or whatever stupid thing you come up with.

Think about it: you play amps now from the Fifties or Sixties that have the original tubes in them, and they sound amazing. That's why there's such a hot market for New Old Stock tubes. But I'm very happy now with my Randall Lynch Boxes with the JJ/Tesla tubes. And it looks like we're moving over to Mullard tubes sometime soon. Good tubes definitely make a difference, but changing them everyday... I don't think so. [*laughs*]

 What's your craziest story from being on the road in the Eighties? —*DOUG SLOAN*

Well, there was the time when I busted my pants out onstage in front of 18,000 people at the Capital Center in Washington, D.C. It was being broadcast on the big basketball screens in the center of the arena. We had just started a song, and we were opening for Aerosmith or Kiss, so we couldn't stop. And I couldn't cover up because just that day I decided to shorten the strap on my guitar so I could be a little more articulate with my playing. I didn't have the coverage I needed, so my roadie ran out with a roll of duct tape and frantically tried to cover things up. It looked kinda cool, but getting the duct tape off, now that was an exercise in pain, dude.

DEAR GUITAR HERO

RICHIE
SAMBORA

OF BON JOVI

You have an incredible guitar collection. With so many to choose from, how do you decide which guitar to play on any given song? —*THE TANK*

Well, Tank, when you've got 135 guitars, it can be a problem. When we tour, I don't bring a lot of my expensive, vintage guitars out with me, 'cause I'm afraid they'll get stolen. Leave a 1959 sunburst Les Paul in a hotel room? I don't think so! [*laughs*] Basically, I have my ESP Richie Sambora signature model, which is very versatile sound-wise. I have a bunch of those. Then I have some Strats, a few Teles, some Les Pauls and Les Paul Juniors. My general attitude is, "whatever fits the song." The vintage stuff I'll use in the studio, but there's certain pieces I'll never take on tour. Why take the risk?

What do you think of Jon Bon Jovi's skills on the guitar? Is he just a simple strummer, or is he capable of busting out a mind-blowing solo?
—*KENNY GRIFFEN*

Jon's been getting better on the guitar. Over the past couple of years, he's really been working on his technique. He never really played any leads until the last tour, and now he's at the point where the two of us are even doing a couple of dual-lead solos onstage. He's always been a terrific rhythm guitar player—very underrated, too, if you ask me.

 On your first solo album, *Stranger in This Town*, **Eric Clapton played on the song "Mr. Bluesman." Did you feel at all intimidated to work with him?** —*HANNAH SMITH*

No, I wasn't afraid at all. I've been fortunate to play with a few of my heroes, and Eric is one of them. He's a very gracious man, very humble, and he never tries to be intimidating. When I was cutting that song, he was playing at the Royal Albert Hall in London, so I went to him so he could record his part. He came down to the studio and blew out a great solo. Afterward, we went to the show together. It turned out to be a great day and evening.

On the song "Superman Tonight," you do a very cool melodic solo. How many passes does it usually take for you to nail a solo? Do you plot them out, or do you tend to go in and wing 'em? —*MICHAEL TYBURSKI*

A little of both. When I plot them out, I just try to get a general framework of how they should go. Otherwise, they tend to sound stale and clinical. Usually I walk in with a basic idea in my head of what the song needs. On that particular cut, I was thinking of a slinky kind of George Harrison–type lead. It didn't take long to lay down. I had a melody in mind, I did a few passes, and it was done. Sometimes I get lucky and I'll be a one-take guy; other times, I have to build solos, particularly if they're long or if I'm trying to find a specific kind of tone. All solos are different, though. They all lead you down a new path.

Q: **I know you're a big Jimi Hendrix fan. Any chance you would ever do an Experience Hendrix Tour? I'd love to see you tear it up with people like Joe Satriani and Eric Johnson.** —*AL RUSSO*

A tour like that sounds great, but I think I'd be more inclined to do my own thing than hop on something where I only get to play a few numbers. But if you can find it, pick up a copy of the soundtrack to [*the 1990 film*] *The Adventures of Ford Fairlane*. I did a version of Hendrix's "The Wind Cries Mary" with Tony Levin on bass and [*Bon Jovi drummer*] Tico [*Torres*]. It's also on the special edition of *Stranger in This Town*, which is unavailable. You can probably catch it on YouTube, though.

Q: **You and Jon have been songwriting partners for a lot of years. What happens when the two of you disagree on a song? Does he automatically win the argument because he's the leader of the band?** —*REBECCA REILLY*

To be honest with you, we rarely have disagreements. I think we've known each other for so long that we kind of know what the other guy is going to like. Songwriting is a give-and-take process, and it can lead to some good, healthy debates. Sometimes it's necessary to push each other out of the comfort zone a little bit. But I would never try to force Jon to record or perform a song he really didn't like. He's gotta sing it, but more than that, he's gotta *feel* it. And you can bet your bottom dollar that if he isn't feeling it, the 80,000 people in the stadium sure aren't gonna feel it either. Jon and I have written something like 400 songs together. If I love a tune and he doesn't, I'll save it for one of my records. Simple as that.

Q: **I saw a picture of you from back in the day, and in it, you're playing a triple-neck Ovation acoustic. Why in the world would you need a guitar like that, and where can I get one?** —*JOHNNY "HANDS" MCQUEEN*

Well, there's only two of them in existence. I used to have both of them, but I traded one for...for something. Wow, I can't remember what I traded it for! As for why I had a guitar like that in the first place, I used to do a solo acoustic interlude onstage before

"Wanted Dead or Alive," and I asked the people at Ovation to build me a special model with a mandolin neck. So you've got the mandolin neck up top, the 12-string neck in the middle and the six-string neck on the bottom. Actually, [Led Zeppelin's] John Paul Jones used to have a guitar with the same neck configuration. I copied him.

 If you could take only one guitar on tour, what would it be?
—EARL ASHTON

I'd have to say my own model, my ESP Richie Sambora model. As I said before, it's very versatile when it comes to the sounds it can deliver. Plus, it's extremely comfortable to play—the balance is perfect, and it's nice and light. And it looks awesome. If I really had to go onstage to play a whole show with just one guitar, I wouldn't have to think too hard about it. As it is right now, I do play most of the set with that guitar. So there you go.

 Les Paul was a great friend of yours. When you think back to the times you two spent together, what's your fondest memory of him?
—DAVID DAMEO

There are a lot of great memories. Most of all, I treasured our conversations, whether they were at my house, his place or in hotel rooms. The friendship we had was very special. I could write a book with the incredible stories he told me. Of course, jamming with him was unbelievable. I played with him at the Iridium [*the Manhattan jazz club where Paul performed every Monday night beginning in 1995*] and before that at Fat Tuesday's [*a famed New York City nightclub that closed in 1995*]. I played with Leo many times, and every time meant something. He was an amazing guy. He was a legend, and he lived long enough to realize he was a legend. What more can you say?

213

DEAR GUITAR HERO

CHRISSIE HYNDE

OF THE PRETENDERS

Q: **After playing, writing and gigging for so many years, do you ever hit the wall musically? And what motivates you to push through that wall?**
—*JIMI MITCHELL*

Do I hit the wall musically? Well, you know, I goof off a lot. I just do music when I feel like it, really. What motivates me? It's just fun to get onstage with the band. I'm not that ambitious, so I don't feel driven to write all the time. I don't agonize over it.

Q: **You've said that James Honeyman-Scott played an influential role in the direction of the Pretenders' sound, but I'm wondering as a guitarist or songwriter what specific things did you learn from him?** —*JOE BAGADONUTZ*

We just complemented each other. He brought the melody out of me, and I got him to rock a little more. I crazied him up a little bit.

Q: **What was your inspiration for [1984's] "Middle of the Road"? Was it based on your experience getting hounded by the press?** —*JEFF RHYMER*

"Middle of the Road" is a reference to the Tao Te Ching, or "The Middle Way" [*a fundamental text of Taoism*]. I've never been hounded by the press. I mean, we need them and they need us, but I've found if you don't court them, then they won't bother you so much.

Q: **From what I understand, Jeff Beck is one of your favorite guitarists. Is it because he's a fellow animal-loving vegetarian, or maybe you admire him for his peerless and inimitable fretboard virtuosity, or maybe it's just his haircut?** —*BRIEN COMERFORD*

Well, he's just a fucking genius. I mean, he's *Jeff Beck*! What's not to love? He's one of the best living guitarists, and he's just a lovely guy. He's been a hero of mine for so many years. I have tried to copy some of his haircuts, but I can't say as much about his playing, since I'm a rhythm guitar player and all.

Q: **I love your use of open chording, like on "Back on the Chain Gang." What other guitar techniques do you feel embody the Pretenders' sound?** —*V. ZUKOWSKI*

Oh, I didn't even know there were open chords. I guess strong rhythm and having players better than me around me characterizes the Pretenders' sound. It's not really about who's the best at what; it's about who does the job.

The Pretenders' rustbelt rock has always reflected and championed blue-collar class values and Midwest life. Does your Akron upbringing and ties to Northeast Ohio still inform your work? If so, how?

—PETE R.

Yeah, it always has. I have that kind of blue-collar/biker mentality. I'm a very ordinary person, and I always feel comfortable with, you know, sitting on a park bench next to whoever happens to be sitting there rather than be with some red carpet people. I don't relate to the celebrity world so well.

Q: As a female guitarist, I'm encouraged by your ability to make it in a male-dominated genre. I'm wondering, what were the highs and lows of being a female guitarist in the music industry back when you started?
—*CHRISTINE*

It was never a problem for me. I had good tunes, and I always brought out the best performances in the people around me. I never thought about it too much. Even during the punk days, it was never too much of an issue. Anyone can pick up a guitar and go. I never felt any discrimination. Actually, I think it was easier back then for me, being that I was the odd one out, or the "novelty."

DEAR GUITAR HERO

ROBB FLYNN

&

PHIL DEMMEL

OF MACHINE HEAD

Phil, why does one of your instruments have polka dots, like Randy Rhoads' guitar? —*MARILYN McCRACKEN*

DEMMEL I started playing maybe a year before [*Ozzy Osbourne's 1980 solo debut*] *Blizzard of Ozz* came out. My first concert was a festival called Day on the Green in 1981, which Ozzy, Loverboy, Pat Travers, Blue Öyster Cult and Heart headlined. Ozzy went on at 10 in the morning and we got there at, like, six to get up front. I remember watching Randy Rhoads play. I was so impressed by how he performed with such passion. He felt *every* note that he was playing. He believed in everything that he was doing. His performance made me admire not only his playing but also the way that he was selling it and the way that he was feeling it. He was such an innovative metal guitar player. You really remember his leads; you can hum his solos. I wanted to incorporate that into my lead playing, especially on *Unto the Locust*. He is a legend, and he was taken too soon. So on my signature guitar, I use [*Rhoads' signature polka-dot*] paint job to pay tribute. I have another one that pays tribute to [*guitarist*] Michael Schenker, 'cause they're my top two dudes.

 "Who We Are" [*from* Unto the Locust] has children singing on it. It's really creepy. What inspired that section, and where did you find the kids? —*GEOFF KRITZ*

FLYNN They're my two sons, Phil's son, and my engineer Juan [*Urteaga*]'s two girls. When I wrote that section, I was playing that intro part on an acoustic guitar and singing those lyrics. My kids were wrestling downstairs—I have a four-year-old and a six-year-old—and they started singing a song just out of nowhere. When I heard it, I thought, Wow, it would be so cool to have this song start off with kids singing.

 How did you get that super-high-gain guitar sound on *Unto the Locust* and keep the notes so clear? —*KEVIN WILLIAMS*

FLYNN I have a [*Peavey*] 5150 amp that I've used forever. I've had him for 14 years and call him "Bubba." I literally have him in a high-security storage area. He comes out to record and then he goes right back in. He never goes on tour. Bubba hasn't been modified at all. It's just one of those magical heads that you come across in your life that stands head and shoulders above the rest. I use that and a Marshall. There is a lot less gain on it than you'd think, and that's part of how we get the clarity and picking definition. A lot of it has to do with my right hand and just being cognizant of my playing. I play all the rhythms, so that really makes it tighter overall. And Phil will come in and do overdubs and leads.

219

Flynn (*left*) and Demmel

You often use natural harmonics to accent riffs, like on "Davidian" from *Burn My Eyes* **and "This Is the End" from** *Unto the Locust*. **How did that technique find its way into your style?** *—JON RICHARDS*

FLYNN When I first started playing guitar, I was really influenced by bands like Black Sabbath, Celtic Frost and D.R.I. Those bands would sometimes do these stops in their songs, where they'd let their guitars feed back. At the time, I was learning how to play on a 45-dollar guitar my dad had rented that came with a little six-inch practice amp. I didn't even know what feedback was. At some point, I stumbled on hitting the harmonic and I thought that was feedback. So when the feedback part came along on a song like Celtic Frost's "Morbid Tales," I would just hit the harmonic. Over time I realized that I had learned it wrong. But as I became a songwriter, I still thought it sounded cool, so I started bringing that into my style. At this point it has become the trademark sound of Machine Head. It's just one of those magical accidents that happens as you're learning, and you just roll with it.

Robb, what piece of gear is the most crucial to your sound and why? *—CARTER BURKE*

FLYNN The Electro-Harmonix Electric Mistress [*flanger*], which is a big old hunking, nine-inch-wide pedal. It's one of the stomp boxes that I use religiously on every album. I use that thing so much, I can't even tell you. It's one of the best pedals ever invented. Listen to the opening riff of "Imperium" [*from 2003's* Through the Ashes of Empires]; that effect is on both the clean part and the heavy part. You can basically hear it in any clean tone on any of our records, like at the beginning of "Aesthetics of Hate" [*on 2007's* The Blackening]. The way that it flanges is unlike any other flange I've found. It's got this watery, glassy tone to it that makes almost anything sound better. I've actually gotta be careful I don't overuse it, because I like it so much.

In your opinion, what is the greatest thrash-metal record of all time? *—JOHNNY D*

DEMMEL Of course there's Slayer's *Reign in Blood*. I was brought up on Slayer; they're the first thrash band I ever saw live. Metallica's *Ride the Lightning* is a great thrash album too. It's probably my favorite Metallica record. And Exodus' *Bonded by Blood* is right up there. So I'm gonna do a three-way tie—a three-headed crown of thrash! [*laughs*]

221

Who is the weirdest musician you have ever met?

—JENNA SWIFT

ROBB FLYNN Dimebag Darrell was a weirdo, in the best way possible! When you were around him, you'd get sucked up into this tornado of lunacy that would take you down these ridiculous paths where you would usually have the best night of your life. He would be like, "We're all gonna paint our beards pink!" And I'd be like, "What?" We toured with Pantera twice, and he was by far one of the greatest characters that I've ever met in my life.

FLYNN The greatest thrash-metal record to me would be *Bonded by Blood*. Growing up in the Bay Area, Exodus were the craziest of all the thrash bands, particularly on that album. Their singer, Paul Baloff, was fucking bat-shit crazy, like a fucking psychopath. When they played shows, he just had this incredible knack for winding up the crowd into a bloodthirsty frenzy. I mean, I've never seen anything like it before or since. Exodus shows back then were the most crazy and violent shows that there were, period.

That record was the soundtrack to my life for years. The first solo that I ever learned how to play was Gary Holt's lead on the song "Bonded by Blood." That record just had such a huge impact on me. Everything about it impacted me: the riffs, the little bit of melody, the attitude. They should have been in the Big Four. They were there, for real, at the beginning.

Q: **Phil, you've talked about how Dimebag Darrell inspired you. What is your favorite Dime story?** —*BRANDON WAGEMANN*

DEMMEL I met Dimebag once at the Download Festival in the U.K. Damageplan were supposed to play right before us. They rolled up, and they'd been on a two-day drinking binge. Dime opened the door to their van and just freaked when he saw us, because he hadn't seen Machine Head since I joined the band. *Through the Ashes of Empires* had just come out, and Dime came up to me. He's all, "You brought the shred into Machine Head. I love your work, brother." It was amazing hearing that from him.

Then I watched him do four more shots before they played, warm up a little bit on Robb's guitar, and go up there and just absolutely kill it live. It was just flawless. That was a couple of months before he passed away. I'm happy I got to share that moment with him and witness him, just to be able to testify that the man was exactly everything he was billed to be.

DEAR GUITAR HERO

STEVE
HOWE

OF YES

Q: **How does it feel to be one of the most amazing guitarists in the history of the instrument?** —*DAVID WILLIAMS*

What's inspired me to be as good as I am is other people. Flavio Sala is a classical guitarist from Italy. When I heard his record, I stopped in my tracks. This is how I describe seeing Albert Lee in 1966. I was playing at Watford Town Hall with Chris Farlowe and the Thunderbirds. Chris comes out to me and says, "I've got a new guitarist, you'd better watch it." So I said, "All right, Chris, I'll be out then." So I'm out there, and when Albert played, I almost fell over. And he had the most penetrating Les Paul Custom sound I've ever heard. Very penetrating. Two pickups on at the same time—*doink!* There's always guys coming along, and when they come along I praise them and say, "This guy knocks me out. Get him on the phone." Flavio came and played in my hotel room when I was on tour in Brazil. That was an honor, a thrill.

Q: **How old were you when you started playing guitar?** —*JASON BOTHAM*

I wanted to start when I was 10. I pestered my parents for two years, and they kept saying, "No, no, no." And I'd say, "Yeah, yeah, yeah." So basically, I started when I was 12, Christmas of that year [1959].

Q: **What's the first song you learned to play on the guitar?** —*JAMIE BLUNDELL*

I think "Apache" by the Shadows was the first thing I did, the first case of "I can play this." At the time, that was the kind of tune you had to know. If you played it like the record, everybody said, "That's great." But I played it at the first concert I ever did, and nobody tuned up, nobody rehearsed it and it sounded dreadful. And I thought I was never going to go onstage again, but then I kind of got into it.

Q: **What's the craziest thing that's ever happened to Yes onstage?** —*ELDON WOLF*

Well, Yes might have had some craziness, but it's not really very crazy. It's more like "twee" crazy. But one day we had a round stage, and it stopped going around. It happened twice, actually. You had to push the bloody thing. We had motors, but quite often the motors failed. Then we had a really big one on the reunion tour [1991], and I think one time that stopped. Nobody pushed that, because you can't push it. You had to fix it. So we actually had to stop the show and go off the stage. That was a pretty big anti-climax.

Q: What are your thoughts on John McLaughlin and Paco de Lucia?
—*DANIEL MICHAEL SERAPIN*

John McLaughlin is just wonderful. I've known about John since about 1965. He was in a group called Geno Washington & the Ram Jam Band, which doesn't sound very John McLaughlin, does it? He was great then and he's still wonderful. I love his warmth and friendliness. And Paco de Lucia—I saw them playing together once. I see them as poles apart because they both invented their own genres, if you like. When Paco came out with that group of his, it was like music had been reinvented. But McLaughlin did the same thing. Mahavishnu was a completely new kind of group. I like them dearly, and you have to be pretty good to be in that bracket.

Q: What do you think of Allan Holdsworth? —*DAVID BEARDSLEY*

Allan is a remarkable guitarist. He plays guitar like he's just been in prison for three years and then he's been let out. He has this marvelous fluidness. I don't know how to talk about the guy, because he's so far out there that he's probably technically the most brilliant guitarist in the world. You have to say, he's kind of jazz. Maybe he doesn't like that word, and most probably it's the wrong word, but he's a wonderful improviser. He's unrivaled.

Q: Will you and Steve Hackett collaborate on another GTR album?
—*HARLEY J. BARNETT*

Will the world ever find peace? [*laughs*] I love Steve, he's a lovely guy. We did GTR, which was a kind of surprise to us both. Somehow Steve and I invented that GTR album by sitting down in a room for three months or something. We really got to know each other and like each other in that writing period. And everything about that record was quite difficult. It kind of went downhill from there. But if Steve and I could imagine another phase of GTR, we'd do it. I don't think we have any restrictions. Of course, Steve is tied up with another member of Yes at the moment: he's done a [*still unreleased*] record with Chris [*Squire*]. Where that's heading when it comes out, what it's called—I don't know.

Q: Ozzy Osbourne once said that Yes had cardboard cutouts of farm animals in the recording studio. Is this true? —*CURTIS ALFELD*

It's partly true. We were making *Tales from Topographic Oceans* [*in 1973*], and we were in a studio called Morgan, and we were there for four months. When we got in the studio, being post-hippie, we needed to make it a bit friendly. Jon said, "I'd like a bathroom to sing in." So he had three walls brought in, tiled, and he sang in a booth with three walls of tiles so it sounded like his bathroom. Jon and I were having a lot of fun. The other guys needed dragging up a hill backward to do this record, because they weren't really sure whether we were too out of it or whether we had a good idea. So anyway, the farm animals weren't cardboard. They were a little more substantial than cardboard. They were like hardboard cows. So, let's correct that: cardboard, no; hardboard, yes.

Q: **What's your favorite breakfast cereal?** —*EVAN CHANDLER*
It's what we call "porridge," but you call it "oatmeal." Obviously, if you get it out of a packet and put it in a microwave, then forget it, it's rubbish. Go to a health store and get some organic oatmeal. If you want to do it the Steve Howe way, it's one cup of oatmeal, one cup of water and one cup of milk. That gives it a nice creamy texture. Don't put sugar in it, on it, or anywhere near the kitchen table. Then get an organic banana. Bananas have to be organic, because everything they spray on bananas goes right through the skin and into the food, and then you're eating pesticides.

Q: **Who do you think are the best prog-rockers since Yes?** —*JOHN ATKINSON*
Dream Theater's John Petrucci is a great example of a continuing prog-rock guitarist. I think Steve Morse is an example. Look what he's done with his band and Dixie Dregs and Deep Purple. He's no ordinary guitarist, that's for sure. I think *prog* should be replaced with "original guitarist." There's a lot of room for originality in this business. In a way, there was a development of music that we had a hand in. Prog was a term; but what that meant was drawing in all influences you can think of—flamenco, jazz, classical. Bring those together—but you're a rock guitarist. That's what the quest was. Anybody who does anything like that is a prog guitarist. I think there's more out there than we realize, like Porcupine Tree.

You and Mick Thomson are known for trading riffs and licks in Slipknot. Do you plan those changes or do they just "happen" in the studio?
—*JAMES LAYGO*

When we recorded [Vol. 3: (The Subliminal Verses)], the trade-offs just happened as we went along. But it doesn't always work that way, and we don't have an established writing method. Even if a song is completely structured before we start recording, it will end up different by the time we're finished because we find ways to improve upon it as we go along. You have to stay open minded and work together to make the song the best it can be.

 What is the weird effect you use during the bridge of "(sic)" in concert?
—*LIAM*

It's a Dunlop Auto Q.

 Which do you think is more important: playing the best you can or putting on a great stage show? Incidentally, you guys strike a great balance. —*DREW*

Do we? Thanks. We try to be as proficient as we can as musicians, but we also want to put on a good show. People sometimes think that we're not really playing because we run samples and loops, so I'll also take this opportunity to say that is definitely not the case.

 You have said that you used to be timid and now you are a freak. So which lifestyle do you enjoy more? —*SHOSHONNA*

Ugh! I never said that. That was something the record label made up for publicity and put on the back of a dumb baseball card, and I always thought it was really stupid. I am what I am, and I've always been a bit of freak—not in any kind of bizarre fetishist way. I'm just rather neurotic.

 There seems to be a lot less anger in your music now. Does success make it harder to write evil, frustration-filled songs like "Eyeless" and "Diluted"? —*TODD*

Yes, to some extent. Your life changes a lot when you have as much success as we've had in such a short amount of time. You look at everything differently. We've been all over the world and seen a lot of different things. We've seen bands come and go and bands

Does wearing a mask while playing in front of thousands of screaming fans make you feel like a different person— or God-like, perhaps? Does it feel different being onstage with Stone Sour as yourself?

—DAVE FROST

I wouldn't say I feel "God-like" wearing the mask, but it is definitely an uninhibitor. And yes, it is an absolutely different experience performing with Stone Sour. The first time I played onstage with them, I felt exposed, like I was trapped in that dream every kid has where you forget to get dressed and go to school in your underwear.

who have been at it for 25 to 30 years and still sound great. Going through all these experiences and seeing the world, you learn a lot about life, music and the music business. Having said that, there is always going to be a tinge of anger and angst in all of us. That's just part of life, which no experience or amount of success can change. But we certainly look at the world differently than when we released our first album.

Q: **Did it bug you to be considered nu-metal?** —*BRIAN*

Yes. I never liked the term or people's apparent need to slap a label on everything they hear. To me, music is just music and I didn't think "nu-metal" was different from any heavy music that came before it. Led Zeppelin wrote metal songs. Even the Beatles wrote heavy tunes.

Q: **What made you guys decide to break out your chops on *Vol. 3*? If you can shred like that, why didn't you ever blow our asses off before?**
—*JOEY NADDEO*

We've always played that way, but the producers opted to edit it out. That's the school of guitar playing Mick and I came from, but it went out of style just because music follows these silly trends, and our producers felt it wasn't necessary for the music. I'm happy and somewhat satisfied to be able to show that side of our playing, but we don't really care if we do it or not, because we've never felt that music is about showing off. Even now, we do it only when the song needs it, and it's hard to figure out how to insert it into some of the old songs, even if, originally, they had more ripping guitar parts. Also, some of our stuff is somewhat tongue-in-cheek. The solo in "Pulse of the Maggots" is a good example. There was a big blank space in the middle of it, and [*producer*] Rick Rubin walked in, put the devil's horn up in the air and said, "This needs some Slayer-style solos." Mick and I looked at each other and giggled. And that's what we gave it.

Q: **Who were the early influences that inspired you to pick up the guitar?**
—*OSCAR MARES*

It's hard to pin them down. My dad had a great vinyl collection and I listened to all of it when I was a kid: the Beatles, Zeppelin, even Billy Squier. That really fired up my love of music. When I first picked up the guitar, at 13, I was really into old Mötley Crüe and Twisted Sister. A few years later I heard Metallica's *Ride the Lightning* and it completely changed the way I looked at guitar playing. After that, I got into all the great speed

What do all of your parents think of your image and careers? Do they brag to their friends about your accomplishments in Slipknot, or do they tell everyone that you are the co-owner of Microsoft?

—JESSE SEIDEL

I can't speak for anyone else in the band, but my mom is completely and totally into my career and always has been. I don't really talk to my dad, but he's into it, too. Both of them were always supportive: they got me my first guitar, my mom bought me my first amp head and my dad drove me to lessons every Wednesday when I was 14. Once, when I was learning a Mötley Crüe song, I warned him that he wouldn't like the music I was playing, and he said, "That's okay. It's your music and you're the one who has to love it." I thought that was very cool.

metal bands that were around in the late Eighties and early Nineties—groups like Flotsam and Jetsam, Anthrax and Death Angel. I cut my chops playing along to stuff like Anthrax's *Among the Living*.

I was in a speed metal band called Atomic Opera and we covered a lot of Metallica, Anthrax and Iron Maiden songs. Playing along to these albums is how I learned guitar and got proficient on it, but I never forgot about guitar players like Jimmy Page, Jimi Hendrix and Steve Howe. They, too, represented a big part of how I wanted to come across as a guitarist. In speed metal, there was so much ego and testosterone that playing a pentatonic lick was frowned upon as being weak, but I always loved it.

 Is the acoustic song "Vermillion Pt.2" played in standard tuning? —*BEN SAMUELS*

It's in C# tuning dropped to B, just like our electric tuning.

 Since all your songs are tuned so far down, why don't you use seven-string or baritone guitars instead of your regular six-string? —*RUSSIAN MAGGOT*

I own too many six-strings to switch. Besides, to add another string to the fretboard would just confuse me. I don't even own a seven-string, though I do want to get one. I'd like a double-neck first, though.

 How do you get those awesome pinch harmonics to come out right every time? —*GAVIN NEUFELD*

It's just from playing guitar for 16 years and practicing. There is no top-secret technique. And, anyhow, they don't always come out perfectly, especially given the low tuning we use. I generally use different picks for harmonics—Dunlop one-millimeter Wedges—and that helps. For intricate picking, intense rhythm pieces and leads I use Dunlop Jazz 3 XL picks.

SYNYSTER GATES
&
ZACKY
VENGEANCE

OF AVENGED SEVENFOLD

You have an incredible live show, with pyro and the works. How much does that set you back a night, and why do you think it's worth it?
—*BILL BROWNING*

GATES It sets us back quite a bit. [*laughs*] Those things are tens of thousands of dollars, and sometimes hundreds of thousands of dollars. But we do it for our fans and for the pride of giving them the best show possible. Yeah, it's a sacrifice, but it's what we set out to do. We put our hearts into everything, not just the music and the records. We do it with the live shows, music videos and everything. We give our all... including money!

VENGEANCE When people spend $30 or $40 on a ticket, they deserve to see something better than normal. They deserve a real cool show. We want to make sure the kids are having a good time.

Like the rest of us, I'm sure as a young guitar player you had dreams of what being a rock star would be like. What is the most unexpected thing about your lifestyle? Did the dreams live up to the reality? —*TERRELL OWSLEY*

GATES It's actually very normal. I was never that obsessed with fame. The money's great. That's kind of what I expected, and it's a really cool thing. I expected to be hassled more, but I kind of just keep to myself. I live right next door to my family members. I have a fiancé, and a little dog that is pretty much our child. Life is pretty normal. Maybe I get a little too drunk sometimes on the road, but that's it.

VENGEANCE I think when you're young and you want to do this for a living, you never really think about all the behind-the-scenes work that goes into it. You just think about playing onstage in front of thousands of people and making lots of money. But I've learned there's a ton of hard work that goes into it. Because, basically, it's still five human beings that have a vision, and it takes a lot of work to realize that vision. If we want something done, we still have to do it ourselves. We still design our merch and our live shows so that they turn out the way we want them to. But it's been fun, and I've learned a lot. I have traveled all across the world, and I've met so many cool people. It's so much more than I could have expected.

What's the worst onstage injury you've ever sustained?
—*PHIL "GRIMLORD" PERRY*

GATES I don't have a "worst" injury, but I can tell you my most embarrassing

You guys have toured the world and played shows with some legends. What's the most memorable thing you've experienced on the road?

—JEFF TODD

GATES Going onstage with Metallica and singing a couple cover tunes with them was a great honor.

VENGEANCE It was definitely playing with Metallica in Berlin, Germany, in front of 80,000 people. I don't get too nervous in front of a crowd, but when you're onstage with Metallica in front of that many people, it's hard enough to remember your own name let alone song lyrics. [*laughs*] We fumbled words and mumbled along, but we had a great time. It was a magical moment.

onstage moment. We were in Montreal playing with System of a Down in front of 20,000 kids. I was up there doing a solo and it was raining, which made everything slippery. I stepped onto one of the metal steps at the front of the stage and slipped right off. It was very embarrassing. I had to watch that one a couple times on YouTube.

VENGEANCE My most debilitating injury would have been on Warped Tour about four years ago. We were playing in Indiana, and it was like 110 degrees. At about the third song in our set our singer, M. Shadows, was swinging his mic and it hit me perfectly on the top of my head. It cut my head right open and the next thing I knew blood was pouring down my face. It was mixing with sweat and going into my eyes and mouth. Because of the heat and the amount of blood I was losing, I started to feel like I was about to pass out. I found this video on YouTube, too. You can see where I start to play the notes all wrong and I'm about to pass out. But I will say that I made it through the whole set, drenched in sweat and blood.

 Syn, you can solo in a bunch of hard rock and metal styles. Are there any exercises or approaches you'd recommend to a young player who's trying to become more versatile? *—ELLIOT SAX*

GATES If you have good picking technique, I think that can apply to everything. You should definitely know a lot of legato, which mostly pertains to metal and distorted playing. If you can do sweep, economy and alternate picking, then you can play acoustic guitar, clean guitar or whatever you pick up. Then it's just all about how you outline the chord changes. With metal you'll likely be staying in, and with jazz you'll be out, but the technique will apply to both.

 You guys not only play some great music but you look good doing it. How important is personal style to Avenged Sevenfold? *—MOLLY SIMMONS*

GATES [*laughs*] I haven't really thought about it, but I guess it's pretty important. My girlfriend designs all the stuff I wear. Her company is called Syn Gates Clothing. I know, it's a very creative name. [*laughs*] Avenged really bump it up when we go onstage, but we don't go walking around town looking like that.

VENGEANCE It's definitely something we take a lot of pride in. I've always been a huge fan of style, whether it's logos or backdrops or clothing. I actually have my own clothing

237

Zacky, you and Syn write some awesome harmonized guitar lines. Do you guys have a typical approach to how you divvy up the parts?

—JT HALSEY

VENGEANCE Syn will come up with something or I'll come up with something, but when we hit rehearsal and start playing them live, that's basically when we decide who will play what. We'll switch around leads and riffs a lot, depending on where our hands are on the fretboard. Syn's an amazing guitar player. He'll often come up with something amazing that just can't be played on 22 frets. And since his guitar has 25 frets he'll obviously be the one to play that part.

company [*Vengeance University*]. And I really think that style is what separates certain bands from the rest of the pack. I've always looked to bands that have good style. No Doubt with Gwen Stefani were always cutting edge, and Rancid and Social Distortion were always looking so cool onstage. I think as long as it feels real, then it's cool. We're always trying to one-up each other onstage, whether it's me wearing bowties or [*bassist*] Johnny [*Christ*] having a Mohawk or coming out in golf knickers. It makes it fun for us.

AL
DI MEOLA

Q: As your career has progressed, how have you come to view life on the road? Is it more or less enjoyable than it used to be? —*COONEY WELLS*

Touring is the only way for a musician to grow artistically. You hone your craft out there, not in a room in a house. You just get better out on the road, because you get the audience's feedback and appreciation. Those are the things that really drive me, and you can't get that sitting around at home. In that respect, touring has become more enjoyable, apart from the physical demands and having no sleep, which is what everybody always complains about.

Q: Can you describe how you play those amazing finger-plucking runs? —*JERRY O.*

The key to whatever is special about my playing probably lies in the rhythm and how I play against the time; and how the time, which is basically the pulse, does not vary against all of the accents that I apply. If you can't keep time and your rhythmic center moves, you run into problems. Technical playing is ineffective without maintaining a sense of time. That's why, whenever I do clinics, I have students tap their feet. If they can't tap their feet against the accents they're playing, then they have to slow the process down until they're able to do it accurately.

Q: Is it frustrating that you're less known to the mainstream public, even though you're in that category of guitarists who are cited as huge influences by other famous players? —*SCOTT M.*

I'm very honored to be considered in that kind of category. I've always played music that knocks me out, and I've always set my standards very high. There were a lot of years after the seminal electric years where I went almost purely acoustic for many records, and I think at that point the ability to reach a younger, up-and-coming audience diminished, primarily because young players in the United States are drawn more to electric music.

Q: Many people regard *Friday Night in San Francisco* [featuring Di Meola, John McLaughlin and Paco de Lucia] as one of the best guitar albums ever recorded. When you were performing during its recording, were you aware that something special was happening? —*DANNY FOGEL*

Oh yeah! That was recorded during something like the last two weeks of a two-month tour. By then, our chops were up. Plus, the three of us were having a ball, and that really

Are you aware that Zakk Wylde sings your praises all the time in guitar magazines?

—J.P.

I'm aware of it. He's a nice guy. I met him at Sony Studios several years back. It's nice to be acknowledged by guys like him who are out in front of a bigger audience than I am.

was heard and seen by the audience. We were complementing one another, but we were also like, Oh yeah? Watch this! It was a really healthy competition.

 You quit Berklee to join Chick Corea's Return to Forever, one of the best fusion bands ever. Is there anything you lost by leaving school?
—*SAL PARKER*

There was always a lot to learn, but I had to weigh that against the experience of playing with musical giants [*including keyboardist Corea and bassist Stanley Clarke*]. Of course I was going to take the opportunity! And it was a dream come true. I remember when Chick called my apartment in Boston and said he wanted me to join the band. He asked me to come down to New York. I packed in 10 minutes and told my girlfriend, "See ya!" I was out the door.

WARREN HAYNES

Q: I am amazed by the depth of your playing across a wide spectrum of music, from blues to hard rock. How deep is your knowledge of theory and how much are you just following your ear? —*RANDY*

I studied a decent amount of theory when I was younger, and I was pretty well versed in it by the time I was 16 or 17. I am less so now, actually. It is important to know that stuff, but the longer you play, the more you naturally realize when theory comes into play and when it does not. It's similar to deciding what and when to play, when to lay back and when to step forward. There are times when playing the blues across certain chords works better than playing fundamentally. You have to use your ear and decide. It's just music; there is no right or wrong. It's just about what sounds good to you.

Q: You perform with Gov't Mule, the Dead, Phil Lesh & Friends and the Allman Brothers Band. How the heck do you go about learning and memorizing all those songs? —*COREY PIKE*

I've always had a knack for being able to remember songs and lyrics, but once that number reaches to 300 or 400, I get a little confused. We learned 168 songs with the Dead before last summer's tour, so I wound up using a modern version of a TelePrompTer, mostly just for lyrics but occasionally also for chord changes and riffs. Between the three bands last summer, there's no way I could possibly keep it all in my head.

Q: What living guitarist have you never jammed with, but wish you could? —*BRENT PRUNER*

There are three: Eric Clapton, who was my first guitar hero; Jeff Beck, who is one of my all-time favorite guitarists; and Carlos Santana, who I've spoken to several times about playing together. We're trying to make it happen.

Q: What is the "Warren Haynes mod" that is performed on Soldano amps? —*KEVIN KERR*

When I first got my Soldano in 1989, I loved the way it sounded, but for some reason I could never get enough bottom end. I called Mike Soldano, who told me the amp was designed to deliver more bottom as the preamp was turned up. Since I was running my preamp at around 3, the amp wasn't delivering what I needed. So Mike added what is essentially a bright switch to the overdrive channel. It actually removes the top end to give a more rounded sound, but only in low-gain settings. The switch lets me choose between the stock sound and the modified sound, but I almost always use the mod setting. If you want your amp that way, you have to call and ask for the "Warren Haynes mod."

Q: **You perform with so many groups. Do you ever put your guitar down?**
—*JAY ROBINSON*

I recently went to Hawaii for two weeks and took only my small Alvarez travel guitar, which I've picked up only three or four times since I got it. It was the first downtime I've had in a long, long time, and it felt good. You have to keep your fingers in shape, but sometimes it's good to give your head a break, and not playing for a while can give your brain a chance to recharge. I had a lot of new ideas afterward.

Q: **Do you find it difficult to perform the vocal and guitar parts simultaneously, since they don't always follow each other rhythmically? It is very difficult to sing on one beat and play on another.** —*JIM WOODARD*

Yes, I do find it difficult. It is hard to perform some of the more complicated pieces with accuracy. It takes a lot of work and concentration, and I find that the less I think about it, the better I am. You have to know the material well enough to be able to perform it without too much thought.

Q: **Your improvisation skills are unquestionable, but do you ever enter the studio with a solo written out? Some of my favorite solos of yours have such a good structure and are so cohesive that they must be composed.**
—*JIM HAGERMAN*

There are certain solos, like "Fallen Down," "Painted Silver Light," "No Need to Suffer" and "Banks of the Deep End," that I play almost the same way every night. In most of those cases, the solo on the record was improvised, but it's stuck in my head and I consider it a part of the song. The only solo I can think of that was fully worked out in advance was in "Fallen Down" [*from Gov't Mule's* Life Before Insanity], which I originally composed as a solo to be played in harmony. [*Producer*] Michael Barbiero convinced me that it sounded better with one guitar, so we let it be.

Q: **In the Allman Brothers Band, did your duties change when Derek Trucks took over for Dickey Betts?** —*JARED WOLFSEN*

I played all the slide parts with Dickey, as did Derek when he performed in the band

with Dickey. As a result, Derek and I were used to playing the same parts on everything: Duane's parts on the old songs and my parts on the newer material. On some songs, it makes more sense for Derek to play my original parts and for me to play Dickey's parts, which took some adjusting. We try to make it fair and democratic and keep each other happy. And one part of that is alternating who plays slide each night on classic songs like "Statesboro Blues," "Dreams" and "One Way Out."

Q: **I've noticed that you play "SlackJaw Jezebel" and "I Think You Know What I Mean" in E♭ tuning with a capo on the second fret. Couldn't you also play that in standard tuning, capo 1st fret? Also, are those awesome slides that you use custom made?** —*JOHN DEVITO*

Good grief! How do you know that? For some reason, a capo on the first fret just feels funny, so I tune down a half step.

The slides are Dunlops that are custom painted on the inside by my guitar tech, Brian Farmer, and his wife Lisa. She does all the swirly, pretty ones. I actually prefer the feel and sound of Coricidan bottles, but they have a closed end, so condensation forms, gets my finger wet and ruins the calluses. That's why I switched to an open-ended slide for live work, though I still use the Coricidan in the studio.

ZAKK WYLDE

Q: **What is your favorite guitar solo out of the songs you have done with Ozzy and Black Label?** —*IAN GIADORNO*

From the Ozzy stuff, I'd say "No More Tears." I did that solo in one take. I wanted to double it and do some other shit, but we ended up just leaving it. It's like my "Stairway to Heaven" solo, because you can *sing* the fucking thing. Really, its whole structure—with the strong melody and the fast thing at the end—is basically a Jimmy Page solo. Ozzy's always loved the "Mama I'm Coming Home" solo. But it's so fucking easy; I could play that solo with a broken hand! For Black Label, I'd pick "New Religion," off *Shot to Hell*. That's a cool solo.

Q: **What inspired you to pick up a guitar?** —*ABE*

For me, it was always about the Les Paul. Jimmy Page played one, and so did Randy Rhoads. When I was young, I remember my buddy Frank had this Les Paul copy. One day he cut apart a package of Gibson strings and taped the Gibson logo across the headstock. We all freaked out, because "Frank had a *Gibson* Les Paul!" [*laughs*] I kid you not, bro. It had Scotch tape on it, but we were so freaked. Frank was the neighborhood god. Actually, not much has changed since then; it's still about the Gibson Les Pauls.

Q: **I know you and Dimebag Darrell were really tight. How did you guys actually meet?** —*MATTHEW LITTLE*

I was in Europe with Pride & Glory [*Zakk's mid-Nineties group*]. We both did the Donington festival, and Pantera just destroyed the place. Aside from Black Sabbath, Pantera are the most powerful band I've ever seen. Dime's playing was beyond sick; the band was pure power. Dime saw me play, too, and after the gig we both came over and complimented each other's playing. That's when we first started becoming buddies. It was like Johnny Winter and Jimi Hendrix: they first dug each other's playing, and then they finally hooked up and became buddies.

Q: **In 1993, you sat in with the Allman Brothers Band at Great Woods for an astounding set. How did that come about? What preparation did you have with the Allmans?** —*TRAVIS GLOTZBACH*

The Allman Brothers' manager, Jonny Podell, knew I was a huge fan. So when something happened with Dickey and he couldn't do the show, Jonny called me. I was in the studio with Ozzy at the time. They flew me out on Saturday night for a show at Great Woods in

Boston the next day. During rehearsal Gregg Allman comes over to me and says in his slow southern drawl, "Yo, Zakk brother, you know how to play fucking 'Dreams,' bro?" And I was like, "Oh, the Molly Hatchet song?" [*laughs*] And he goes, "Man, another comment like that and we're gonna have to send you back home." [*laughs*] They hate Molly Hatchet! And I'm talking about Molly Hatchet to the guy who originally wrote that amazing song!

But the show was cool as shit, man. To me, it sounded like Mahogany Rush playing with the Allman Brothers. [*laughs*] It was hilarious. After the first show, they were like, "We love you Zakk. Now get the fuck outta here." I guess the Molly Hatchet and Frank Marino shit didn't go over too well. [*laughs*]

Q: **What is your favorite guitar album and why?** —*TIM GREGG*

The list is endless, but if you wanna hear sick guitar playing, *Friday Night in San Francisco* [*a 1980 live album with Al Di Meola, John McLaughlin and Paco de Lucia*] is the record to buy.

Q: **I love your music and your look, especially your beard of doom. How long did it take to grow? Do you have any grooming secrets?** —*MIKE*

Just let it go, man. Who gives a shit. Don't cut it. The reason I started growing the beard was because I was tired of shaving every day on the road. Actually, Ozzy wanted me to cut it, but I was like, "Ozz, I'm not Justin Timberlake and I'm not 19 years old. I'm a grown man. I don't like hanging out with teenage girls." [*laughs*] Then I was like, "Let's see how gay and stupid this beard can get." So the guys and I started having a contest to see who could grow the biggest, stupidest beard. I'm the only one who still has it, so I guess I won the douche bag award! [*laughs*]

Q: **You and Dime had many adventures, but if you had to choose just one, what would be your favorite memory of Dimebag?** —*DON BESS*

Definitely us in the truck. That was the fucking best. I was driving and Dime was in the passenger side. I ran over, like, 10 stop signs, fences, a park…we were going, like, 20 miles an hour and slamming it into reverse and then back into gear. I thought the car was a rental, but it was Dime's manager's wife's car! [*laughs*] She had bought it the day before! That was some quality shit. We were so stealth that we left a trail of broken shit and mailboxes that led right into Dime's fucking house! When the cops came down, they

What was your most embarrassing moment onstage?

—RAZZ

There can't be any embarrassing moments. I'm pathetic! [*laughs*] My whole life is an embarrassment. It's like George Costanza, bro. [*laughs*]

already had the license plate…because it had fallen off the front bumper. [*laughs*] That was beyond gay hysterical, bro.

Q: **How much can you bench?** —*JOEY GIORDANO*

I'll throw, like, 275 on there. That's about as heavy as I'll go, because sometimes I feel like I'm getting tendonitis in my elbows. I'm definitely not throwing 500 pounds up there. But I tell my wife all the time, "Sweetie, I bench 805, and I've got a 15-inch cock." [*laughs*]

Q: **I'm a big fan of Randy Rhoads' crazy solos. How do you remember long solos like "Mr. Crowley"? Any memory tips?** —*BEN MERCHANT*

Keep drinking beer. [*laughs*] Through my experience dealing with Ozzy and having a wife and three kids, I've discovered that beer improves the memory…and heals the pain!

Q: **When you first joined Ozzy's band, you looked like the next Fabio! I bet you were pulling tons of chicks. Do you find you attract a different kind of woman now that you look like a dirty biker?** —*KIRSTEN PYLE*

You mean since I've been working at the gay brothel? [*laughs*] I've been attracting some shit I don't even have the words to describe!

Q: **What is the most important element in achieving your tone?** —*STEPHEN HENCKE*

Well, the good Lord obviously gives you certain gifts, but what you do with them is really up to you. You gotta apply yourself. I don't care how much talent you got. It's like if you're a baseball player: if you don't take batting practice, stay healthy and work your ass off, you're never gonna reach your potential. You can always get better on the guitar, but you gotta constantly practice. There is *no* substitute for hard work, I don't care how good you are. You could be the heavyweight champ of the world, but if you ain't training, you're gonna get your ass kicked. Same with the guitar: if you lose your drive, you're done.